D0547483

else's I can lay my hands on) to add to the compost all winter and into the next year.

The truly great thing about gardening is that there are certain universal principles that work for all gardeners everywhere:

One: Know your microclimate. That's your neighborhood, your own backyard, set within the general hardiness zone of your region. Mainly, it's a strong intimacy with your own backyard that will tell you when it's safe to plant seeds, bulbs, perennials, even trees. It doesn't matter how far north you live, there are features that link you with other gardeners. In the very far north, for instance, a short growing season in number of days is compensated for by the extra length of those days. Northern gardeners can grow pretty much the same annuals and perennials as more southerly gardeners.

Two: All gardening is an experiment. Keep trying plants that are slightly out of your zone just to see how far you can push the limits of your gardening. The hardiness of a plant is measured by its tolerance

The third section is what I call Le Jardin des Refusés. Like the salons rejected artists used, it holds anything I can't deal with anywhere else. It's a cutting garden, a holding zone, an experimental area. It has Japanese maples, small shrubs, trees, ornamental grasses and dwarf evergreens. There is a large wooden compost situated near the back. I can see the front garden from my office window. It's designed as a tapestry of hostas, ground covers and small shrubs and trees. And it looks good enough from the sidewalk to make people stop and make notes.

I've had this same plot of land since 1967 and have never used chemicals. I'm lucky enough to live in a neighborhood where much the same attitude is held by everyone. So no clouds of poison come wafting about on the breeze or infect the soil.

I never dispose of anything from the garden unless it's diseased. It all goes into the compost. I seldom cultivate because I top dress all the plants with a combination of compost and manure with leaf mold added. I store leaves from my garden (and anyone

Introduction

19 ft/5.7 m wide by 130 ft/39.6 m deep in the back, and 19 ft/5.7 m by 40 ft/12 m in front. To organize the design I created three very distinct spaces: Closest to the house there's a hot spot (six hours of sun on a good day) shaped by 2 ft/60 cm square paving stones set centrally in checkerboard style. I grow herbs and other plants that love all the heat the stones retain; the north- and south-facing fences each have slightly different microclimates, and therefore the borders fronting them have very different kinds of plants.

The central section contains a berm made of sod ripped up from every part of the property, then turned over to compost. It was planted intensely with shade-loving plants. This woodland section is under the high canopy of a gigantic weeping willow tree in the neighbor's garden. This is a very difficult tree to garden around, since it has a voracious appetite for food and water as well as very shallow roots. Yet this doesn't seem to bother the hundreds of plants that live all around.

INTRODUCTION

Gardening is the great obsession of my life. Since I'm a professional gardening writer, my garden has to suit many different needs as well as moods. I can't walk through the garden without thinking about the intense life that's going on beneath my feet.

When people come into my garden they invariably say, "It must be a lot of work." I don't think so. It's a joyous pastime; it is also part of my work. It is my library, my instructor, my companion. When you learn so much new stuff every day, the excitement supersedes the concept of labor or even heavy work. As I've gotten older, I now get help but like all obsessed gardeners, I've worked out my own fussy way of doing things.

First of all, let me describe just what I have. It's a small glorious garden on a downtown lot measuring

Acknowledgments

Thanks to Juliet Mannock and Alix Davidson for invaluable advice, tips and editing suggestions for this edition. And to Nadia Bobak who edited this version so skillfully.

Material designated with ** may only be available in the U.S. or through on-line retailers.

DISCLAIMER

Never use a plant medicinally without consulting a professional. Self-medication is always risky.

ACKNOWLEDGMENTS

Many of the tips in these pages have appeared in my garden column for *The Globe and Mail*. I am grateful for the privilege of writing this column and for its truly fascinating audience. Their letters and ideas are always informative and fun to read. I've incorporated material from them as well. It's been my pleasure to work with Sarah Murdoch, and Sheree-Lee Olson, both superb editors.

Major thanks go to Jacqueline Rogers, who worked on the first edition of this book. And to Tom Thomson, a former Horticulturalist at Humber Nurseries in Toronto, and one of the smartest gardeners I've ever met. The other gardeners whose ideas I gleaned include: Gerry Fichtemann, Cheryl Grigg, Mildred Wills, Art Laurenson, Reg Curle, Cadwell Tyler, Jean and Philip de Gruchy, Heather Ross and Sylvia Rouble.

Canadian Garden Tips

© 1994, 2003 by Marjorie Harris. All rights reserved.

Published by HarperCollins Publishers Ltd

No part of this book may be used or reproduced in any manner
whatsoever without the prior written permission of the publisher,
except in the case of brief quotations embodied in reviews.

First published in paperback by HarperCollins Publishers Ltd 1994.
Pocket paperback edition 1998. Second paperback edition 2003.
This Collins Gem® paperback edition 2004.

Collins Gem® is a registered trademark of HarperCollins
Publishers Ltd (UK).

HarperCollins books may be purchased for educational, business, or
sales promotional use through our Special Markets Department.

HarperCollins Publishers Ltd   www.harpercollins.ca
2 Bloor Street East, 20th Floor
Toronto, Ontario, Canada
M4W 1A8

Illustrations by Kveta

National Library of Canada Cataloguing in Publication is available

TC 9 8 7 6 5 4 3 2 1

Printed and bound in Canada

Collins Gem

Canadian Garden Tips

Marjorie Harris

HarperCollins*Publishers*Ltd

5-08

for cold, drought, wind, sun, type of soil and length of growing season. A zone will give some idea of the annual minimum temperatures but doesn't take into account everything else. You can't necessarily grow a banana tree in the Arctic, though I'm sure there are those trying it in a special microclimate somewhere; as well, some plants that grow in moderate areas will shrivel up and die in a hot climate. My rule of thumb is to try any plant (at least the ones I absolutely long for but really am not supposed to be able to grow) at least three times before giving up. Plant it in a new spot each time—where the soil is slightly different, the wind conditions more amenable, the drainage slightly faster (or more sluggish, depending on the plant's cultural needs). Never be intimidated by what seem to be Carved-in-Stone rules. Most of them can and will be broken by the adventurous. But don't be foolhardy. It really is impossible to grow desert plants in a rainforest, or woodland plants in full sun. However, sun lovers will grow in shade but they will be lax and won't bloom.

I ignore most rules by default once in the garden, and nothing else interferes. I generally overlook exactly when you are supposed to move plants and keep them in what seems like perpetual motion—but not in the midst of a heat wave or when a hard frost is imminent. There are some mini rules such as keeping them in the shade for a while after planting, and babying them along with water and compost—just a bit of extra attention. So what if a plant dies? There's always room for something new and exciting in the empty holes.

I raid all other gardens for ideas whether they are public or private. I'm almost never disappointed. One of my greatest pleasures is talking to other gardeners as I travel. They are invariably generous with their ideas and plants. So my garden is filled with references to their magnanimity. And so is this book.

The tips included here are of two kinds. Most of them are ones I use in my own garden and have worked well for me over the past few decades of gardening. Others I've collected from many different sources—from magazines (I'm an inveterate clipper, though not a very good filer), from books, from other gardeners—especially from other gardeners. I haven't used some of the tips myself because they aren't relevant to my kind of gardening or area. But I pass them along because they are enchanting and have the backing of gardeners who have used them with success.

The tips are organized in alphabetical order because it has always been my fantasy to have the tips I need—and can never find when I want them most urgently—ready to hand.

Gardening should be fun, and I hope a lot of these tips will provide some amusement as well as being useful. There are lots of lurid-sounding homemade mixes for killing off bugs, weeds and diseases, as well as ideas for feeding the plants you want to keep. These follow the precept I always use: to garden ecologically. That is, to use only organic methods. To keep away from chemicals that might in some way damage the soil or the water table or harm birds and beneficial bugs and bacteria.

Gardening should be going with nature, not against it. Once you have healthy plants and soil, not only will your plants be stronger and more able to withstand any onslaught of disease or munching on by unwanted pests but you'll feel better as well.

We are not making enough connections between what we spread on our lawns and the effect on small animals and children. I've heard horror stories about beautiful suburban areas where the lawns are gorgeous and green and kept that way with chemical intervention. Most of the children on the street have allergies and are prone to colds and sickness. The adults don't feel very well either. It's hard to believe that we are doing this to ourselves.

It isn't harder or more time-consuming to garden ecologically, but when we learn to respect nature and follow natural laws, we will make gorgeous gardens.

ACID SOIL

We always yearn for what's hard to get in gardening—most of us want acid-loving plants such as rhododendrons and azaleas even if we have completely neutral soil. If you decide to adjust the pH of the soil to accommodate ericaceous plants, make sure that you change it over a wide area. Otherwise, once roots make it out of the zone of change they will be in soil that is likely to cause stress.

* Soil is slowly being acidified by the persistence of acid rain in certain areas—a good reason to get your soil tested to see where your pH stands.

* To make soil more acid, put rinds of lemons, limes and oranges through a food processor and bury them in the soil; add your coffee grounds as well. This method is slow, but you do make steady progress over the years.

* To neutralize soil, collect cast-off drywall scraps and crush them with a hammer. Soak in water. The lime in the drywall will raise the alkalinity and thus the soil pH. Make it fairly dilute so no chalky spots are left behind. Shake as you pour to prevent the lime from settling. Use this solution on mossy spots on the lawn, or in the garden, or wherever else there are indicators that the soil is too acidic.

* As a stop gap pour ½ cup water plus ½ cup vinegar around the dripline and water in. See also pH; Soil.

Aging

When stones or rocks look aged, they appear to have been in place forever. It gives a settled effect to a new garden and adds solidity to an old one. Here are some methods of making an instant patina—well, almost instant . . . at least it won't take years. It's important to repeat the process after each rain until you get the desired effect.

* Blend half and half live moss, preferably one that's already been growing in cracks in the sidewalk, with either beer or buttermilk in an old food processor or blender. Paint it on the surface.

* Mix half and half live culture yogurt with either beer or buttermilk.

* Make a paste (a slurry) of cow manure and water and paint it on new walls or stone. One of my hort-buddies, on a trip to a famous garden in England, watched the gardeners there tarting up a new wall with this to blend the old and the new.

* Paint on plain yogurt (the acidulous form). Once the moss takes hold you can ignore it, even in drought.

See also PATINA.

ALCHEMILLA MOLLIS

Lady's mantle flops over elegantly to soften paths and disguises the mess left behind by withering bulb leaves, or in drifts in boring spots. It holds the last drop of dew in its velvety leaves.

* Cut off the acid yellow flowers close to the soil, hang upside down for a couple of weeks and use in dried flower arrangements. I especially like these combined with the blooms of dried peonies.

* An infusion made with the leaves helps with skin inflammations, acne and freckles (it's supposed to make them less obvious; being a freckled person, I think they are beautiful as they are). Always be careful when using any plant for medicinal reasons.

* Be sure to whack them right back almost to the ground after they've bloomed. They will sulk for a while, but the new growth is so delightful it's worth the wait.

Allelopathy

Allelopathy is the production by one plant of substances that inhibit the growth of another. In some
species, rain washing over the leaves will leach the
inhibiting substance into the soil. This is true for
hemlock. For this reason, never use hemlock
branches or needles for mulch.

* Allelochemics is the study of the chemical interac-
tions between species.

* Pheromones are substances secreted from and sent
to another in the same species with very specific mes-
sages. Sex pheromones, for example, are released by
insects as a form of mating call.

* Allomones cause a plant, insect or animal to do
something beneficial for itself, such as create protective
venoms or produce prey and pollination attractants.

* Kairomones are toxins that are detrimental to surrounding plants. For instance, black walnut and some
maples tell other plants not to grow around their roots.
On the other hand, English walnut doesn't mind.

ANNUALS

Any garden is lacking without some annuals; I only object to gardens planted *entirely* of annuals. They are plants that complete their life cycle—germinate, flower, form seeds and die—in one season. But they have a very valuable function in the garden; for instance, they can fill in holes left after bulbs have been moved to ripen.

Some of my favorite annuals: *Bacopa* spp; *Calibrachoa* hybrid; *Petunia* 'Surfina', 'Million Bells'; *P.* 'Purple Wave', 'Pink Wave' and 'Fantasy Blue'; *Coleus* 'Inky Fingers', 'Golden Bedder'; *Osteospurmum* 'Lemon Symphony'; *Rudbeckia* 'Cherokee Sunset'; *Zinnia* 'Dreamland Yellow'.

* Plant hardy annuals before the last frost. Many of them will self-sow to keep the breed going. *Coreopsis*, tickseed; *Cynoglossum amabile*, Chinese forget-me-not; *Dianthus chinensis*, Chinese pink; *Calendula officinalis*, pot marigold; *Centaurea cyanus*, cornflower, bachelor's buttons; *Eschscholzia californica*, California

poppy; *Gaillardia pulchella,* blanketflower; *Helianthus,* sunflower; *Lobularia maritima,* sweet alyssum; *Portulaca grandiflora,* moss rose; *Viola pedunculata, V. tricolor,* Johnny-jump-up; *Consolida,* larkspur.

* Hardy but not self-sowers: *Tropaeolum majus,* nasturtium.

* Half-hardy seeds can be planted after the last frost but before the warm weather sets in permanently—they like cool, not cold, conditions. Cosmos self-sows; *Rudbeckia hirta* 'Gloriosa Daisy', black-eyed Susan and *Salvia splendens,* scarlet sage, can be grown in part shade.

* Tender annuals have to be started indoors, or planted only when there is absolutely no danger of frost.

* Annuals that can be planted as soon as the soil is workable in spring: bachelor's buttons, calendula, gaillardia, larkspur, phlox, portulaca, sweet alyssum, sweet pea.

* Sow annuals close to relatives (larkspur beside delphinium) so they can be a similar substitute.

Antidesiccant Spray

Usually used to protect evergreens from being dried out by winter winds and sun, it can also be used as an organic fungicide. Spray plants prone to mildew, such as lilacs, in early spring.

* The commercial products protect trees and shrubs from wind burn—a big problem in the winter. We keep forgetting that woody plants, especially evergreens, continue to transpire during the winter. Of course, these products also work during prolonged periods of drought.

* Dip bulbs and tubers in this stuff to help preserve them for winter storage. Add water to a brand such as Wilt-pruf and use in a spray bottle.

Ants

Ants can be really annoying, especially if they decide to build a colony in the middle of your favorite bed.

They do have a good side, which is sometimes hard to remember—they aerate the soil and many are crucial to moving seeds about. Some species control pests such as caterpillars in orchards. If, however, you have too many:

* Try the following: blend orange peel with a little juice to make a thick paste. Pour over ant hills, making sure some goes into the holes. This should get rid of the ants in a few weeks. Apparently, oranges give off a gas the ants cannot tolerate.

* I have friends with cottages who swear that cucumber parings near ant runs deflect them away from buildings.

* Plant tansy in the garden and sprinkle the dried flowers around the doors to keep ants out of the house.

* If ants are bothering one of your plants, put a bit of Vaseline on the base of the stem and they'll leave it alone immediately.

* Leave half-cut lemons on their runs indoors—they hate them.

See also PEONIES.

Aᴘʜɪᴅs

In spring, ants round up aphids, move them to spots where the aphids can feast on the delicious new leaves, then they milk the aphids for the sweet nectar they produce. Green, black, pink, yellow and red aphids will attack just about anything and deform leaves. Plant nasturtiums around the garden to attract the aphids away from other plants. Then pick off the infected plants and get rid of them.

* Chives between sunflowers and tomatoes will perform the same function.

* Ladybugs eat aphids by the thousands. To attract them, plant nasturtiums, Queen Anne's lace, marigolds or goldenrod.

* Except for its edible stalks, rhubarb is poisonous to people, but it's also anathema to aphids. Try this spray:

> 3 lb/1.3 kg rhubarb leaves
> 4 qt/4 L water
> 1 oz/28 g laundry soap flakes

Chop rhubarb leaves, add 3 qt/3 L water, simmer for 30 minutes. Cool and strain. Dissolve soap in remaining water, stir into rhubarb and water mixture. Spray on roses against black spot.

* Yellow is incredibly seductive to aphids. Fill a bright yellow pan with soapy water and leave it in the garden to entice them in where they will drown.

* Place crumpled shiny aluminum foil around stems of vulnerable plants. The brightness confuses aphids and discourages them from hanging around.

* Natural insect predators: aphidius wasp; green lacewing larva; ladybug.

* Spray aphids with natural botanical sprays that include insecticidal soap, or any other soap spray.

ARTEMISIAS

Easy to care for, artemisias love lots of sun and will tolerate drought. Bar none, they are my favorite plants. The glorious silver and gray foliage acts as a foil to other colored leaves. Use them to knit disparate parts of the garden together or to provide a wave of contrasting foliage with brightly colored leaves and blossoms.

* Weave gray foliage through the garden as punctuation marks to stop the eye from wandering over the scene without really seeing the plants. Create beautiful sentences with your plants.

* *Artemisia absinthium*, wormwood, is so useful I could not imagine a garden without it. Chop up the leaves in autumn and make an infusion—pour hot water over them, and let sit for an hour or so to cool off. Strain, and pour the tea around plants such as hostas that are horribly affected by slugs. This helps kill off overwintering beasts.

* *A. abrotanum*: Dry and hang in bags in closets to

prevent moths. Burn in fireplace to remove cooking odors. Plant near cabbages to protect from cabbage worm butterfly and near fruit trees to protect from fruit tree moths.

* *A. pontica* is considered hideously invasive, but I find it makes a wonderful low-growing hedge. Define how far you want it to go in the spring and then whack it back a couple of times during the season to keep it nicely in place. Throw the detritus into the compost.

* *A. cineraria* as a border will keep animals out of the garden. Repels moths, flea beetles and cabbage worm butterfly.

* *A. lactiflora* and *A. vulgaris*, two varieties similar to each other, but the latter is often considered a weed. These plants repel lice. They exude a toxic substance into the soil around them that remains active for a fairly long time. Don't plant near fruit trees because they retard growth in surrounding plants.

Asparagus

Once you've had your fill of asparagus as a vegetable, leave the stalks to become fine feathery fern-like plants. They are decorative in the garden and in flower arrangements. In fall, when they finish turning yellow, cut them right back to the ground. Then mulch.

Unfortunately, they also attract the asparagus beetle. It's a prolific little beast that produces disgusting black larvae. Plant tomatoes near your asparagus to discourage these guys. Never cut down the frond until it looks too droopy and despairing as they need this top growth to make next year's spear.

Autumn Color

I love the rich textures and smells of autumn. This is when annuals really shine: browallia, lantana, globe amaranth, ageratum, impatiens, nicotiana and cleome.

Perennials include just about every aster and any Michaelmas daisy I can get my hands on; *Eupatorium maculatum*, Joe-Pye weed; *Anemone japonica*, Japanese anemone; *Tricyrtis*, toad lily; *Ceratostigma plumbaginoides*, plumbago—a glorious ground-cover with cobalt blue flowers and foliage that turns crimson. Of course, as many forms of sedum as possible, especially *Sedum spectabile* 'Autumn Joy'. *Pennisetum alopecuroides*, fountain grass; and *Imperata cylindrica* 'Red Baron', Japanese blood grass.

* Some autumn annuals that can be planted as soon as the soil can be worked in spring: bachelor's buttons, calendula, gaillardia, larkspur, phlox, portulaca, sweet alyssum, sweet pea. Many of them will also self-seed in warmer areas.

* Trees and shrubs for glorious autumn foliage: *Acer palmatum*, Japanese maple, in all sizes, shapes and forms; *Euonymus elata*, the famous burning bush of almost scarlet neon intensity; *Enkianthus campanulatus*, redvein enkianthus, turns an especially deep scarlet; *Ligustrum*, golden privet; *Betula*, birch, in any form.

Azaleas

One of the most common mistakes when planting azaleas is to plant too deeply. Unless you're planting in light, sandy soil, plant with the top of the azalea's root ball just barely at the soil's surface. So roots aren't exposed, cover with loamy organic matter—leaf mold or compost. Mulch with pine bark or needles.

BACILLUS POPILLIAE

Milky spore disease is a bacterial organism that produces a disease in the grubs of Japanese beetles. Apply 1 tsp/5 mL to sections 3 ft/1 m apart to the soil on a still day.

BACILLUS THURINGIENSIS

Bt is an insecticidal bacterium that will dry up anything it hits, including your skin. Be careful when you use this stuff. Don't breathe it in—wear a mask. Once applied, it isn't toxic to animals or plants but can be used against tent caterpillars and on vegetables such as cabbage, broccoli and other brassicas.

BAREROOT PLANTS

Bareroot plants must be planted while they are still dormant. Nurseries often ship bareroot stock to save on express charges. They are delicate and very likely to succumb to shock, which is why it's so important to get them into the soil quickly.

* Soak the roots to revive them, then put them into a well-prepared hole. To prepare the hole: Dig the hole three times as wide as the plant, and the same depth as the roots. Water the hole well; make sure there is good drainage. Pop in the plant, fill the hole with soil, water again. Once the water has drained, top dress with a layer of compost or sheep manure. For more planting instructions, see PLANTING.

BASIL *Ocimum basilicum*

Basil is my favorite culinary herb. It's so versatile, I like to plant as many as I possibly can. Plant it in pots, among perennials, alone or as a companion plant. Pinch out the tops to make them shrubby, thus producing more leaves for eating. For better flavor, pinch off flowers. This will also extend leaf production.

* Planted around tomatoes, basil helps them ward off insects and disease.

* Design a basil bed: Start at the edges with a purple form such as 'Ruffles', 'Rubin' or 'Dark Opal'; back these up with 'Cinnamon' and 'Anise', a paler purple; then 'Green Ruffles' with lime green foliage and serrated edges. By combining ornamental and edible basils, you can make a beautiful herbal knot garden. To add variety, plant different types of parsley.

Bay Leaf *Laurus nobilis*

Bay is an elegant plant in pots. My area is too cold to leave it in the garden all winter, but it is a striking plant to prune into a standard for a large container. For a formal effect, select a plant with a straight central stem, keep all the leaves except those at the top from developing and shape it into a ball.

* Add rosemary to the same pot along with *Helichrysum petiolatum*.

* A bay leaf in grains and flours protects them against insects and weevils.

Beans

Don't plant beans near garlic or chives, which inhibit the beans' growth. They do well planted with beets, cucumbers and cabbages.

* Beans fix nitrogen in the soil, so leave the roots behind when you finish harvesting. Cut the plants down to ground level; let them compost into the soil ready for a new crop of vegetables next spring.

* Examine bean seeds carefully—they have a little spot on one side where the root emerges. Plant spot side down for more rapid growth.

* Marigolds are said to ward off Mexican bean beetle.

* Plant climbing beans to grow up the stalks of corn, which will act as an anchor and also keep them out of reach of raccoons.

BERMS

One of the best things I did in my garden was to make a berm in the center of one area. Try one in either a front or back garden if you have a deadly boring flat surface. Make sure it is in scale with the entire lot and doesn't look like some sort of pimple on the landscape (too small) or a looming ogre (too large). A decent size berm stands about 4 feet/1.2 meters high.

* This is an excellent way to recycle material. Form the base with rocks or detritus such as broken-up cement. Cover with soil.

* I used all the sod I pulled up when I remade my garden—a really good use for grass. I turned the sod over, let it compost down, then planted *Lysimachia nummularia*, creeping Jenny, a fairly benign but

fast-moving ground cover that grows in sun or shade to hold the soil in place.

BINDWEED *Convolvulus arvensis*

This is the most virulent of all creeping vines. It strangles everything in its path and has a 10 ft/3 m root system that sends out runners that stretch from 3 to 10 ft/1 to 3 m long. Keep cutting off the tops until the roots die of starvation.

* Don't try to pull this weed out; it will inevitably break off and form new plants. The minute you see it emerge, cut off at ground level; eventually you will starve the roots.

BIOLOGICAL SPRAYS

These are any organic sprays that help get rid of aphids, June bugs, black spot and fungus diseases.

Rhubarb is a terrific base for a homemade spray. This spray will keep in a cool dark place for a few months.
* Steep six rhubarb leaves in 2 to 3 qt/2 to 3 L boiling water; strain. Cool before using. Don't reuse pot for cooking meals.

BIRCH *Betula*

Birch trees speed up the decaying process of compost if you site the pile about 6 ft/2 m away.
* Plant *Sanguinaria canadensis*, bloodroot, at its feet for a glorious effect.
* Buy your local native birch, which are not prone to birch borer and fungal diseases as are European birches.

BIRDS

Attract birds to your feeder with this inexpensive treat: Fill a 2 cup/500 mL plastic container with sunflower seeds and store in the fridge. Every time you pour fat off any meat dish, pour it into the container (make sure it's not so hot that it melts the container). When the pot is full, remove the-fat-and-seed ball from the container and put it on the feeder.

* Plants and shrubs that attract birds and provide shelter: elder, mulberry, cotoneaster, Russian olive, hawthorn, honeysuckle, dogwood, *Amelanchier*. Evergreens are great nesting spots.

* To keep birds away from newly seeded beds, hang shiny objects, such as bits of mirror or aluminum foil, from bamboo poles placed randomly about.

* A cheap way to keep birds away from seedlings or off ripening fruit is to use good old-fashioned Christmas tree tinsel. Tie the tinsel to stakes pushed far enough into the soil so the tinsel is just about ground level for newly seeded beds or a few inches/centimeters above strawberries.

* Use clothespins to fasten tinsel to berry bushes or cherry trees about every 3 ft/1 m.

Bone Meal

A powder of ground-up animal bones that is rich in phosphorus and, to a lesser degree, nitrogen. Adding it to soil is a very old method of providing these nutrients. It supplies food for blossoms and reduces acidity in the soil. Find the source—there is always a worry about mad cow disease.

Borage *Borago officinalis*

This attractive herb with aromatic leaves and bright blue flowers self-seeds like crazy and generally disports itself around the garden in a most pleasing way. It attracts bees to the garden, and its leaves provide calcium, potassium and trace minerals to compost so be sure to add them.

Borers

They may look like flashy green, black and red wasps, but they are probably borers. In the larval stage the squash borer is a destructive little pest. You'll be tipped off to its presence when the plants get hit with wilt. The cycle of this Eastern native is: eggs turn into caterpillars with brown heads; moths emerge from the caterpillars and burrow into squash stems. A light row cover over plants in early spring will keep the adult from laying eggs. It will also keep out leafhoppers and squash beetles.

* Squash borers and peach borers are related; they appear in June and July.

* Botanicals: Rotenone will kill young larvae, but may also mess up the ecology of your garden. Inject an infected plant with Bacillus thuringiensis (Bt) instead.

* Get rid of any infected vines and turn the soil deeply in spring. Put a plastic mulch over the area.

* Plant nasturtiums around fruit trees to repel borers.

* Plant anything in the onion family (chives, alliums, garlic) around fruit trees.

BOTANICAL SPRAYS

Confusion arises about the difference between natural poisons derived from plants and those created by chemicals. The former are botanicals and used by nature; the latter are manufactured and we do not always know their wide-ranging effects. The leaves of rhubarb, for instance, are poisonous and make a useful spray for vegetables; it will kill bugs but won't kill people. On the other hand, to eat rhubarb leaves might be fatal.

* Look for the following on containers to find out if they are organically correct:

* Some roots produce a natural insecticide. For an effective spray, soak the rhizomes of hellebores overnight, crush, boil, and strain.

* Ruta (rue): The very bitterness will deter Japanese beetle from roses and raspberries.

* Ryania: Paralyzes insects. Ryania is a tropical plant.
* Sabadilla: When heated, seeds are toxic to many insects. See SABADILLA.
* Pyrethrum: From the flower of the same name from the chrysanthemum family. Dry the flower, crush it to a powder and mix with water. It's easier to buy it commercially—just read the label, and follow the instructions.
* Oil sprays: Dormant oil sprays are effective in orchards and against sucking and chewing insects. They suffocate larvae, but must be applied before the blossom season.

BOULDERS

If you use boulders or large stones in your landscape, make sure that each is from one- to two-thirds underground depending on the size. This will make them appear as though they are slowly rising from the primordial earth. Boulders scattered about without

concern for a natural effect are dreadful. I call it ston-
ing the environment.

* Always have a reason for putting in stones, rocks
and boulders. And use them in moderation. A river of
rocks can be handsome in the right location, but
strewn around trees and lawns mindlessly doesn't
make much sense.

BRASSICAS

This family of vegetables includes cabbage, cauliflower, broccoli, collards, kale and turnips. Hyssop,
wormwood and southernwood nearby keep away the
white cabbage fly. Plant aromatic herbs such as dill,
sage and peppermint near them. Compost heavily.
Mulch when the weather is dry.

* If the heads of these plants are too small, they can
probably be improved with the addition of lime,
phosphorus or potash to the soil.

* Plant broccoli seeds directly into the soil in July for a

fall crop. When you harvest the main stalks (heads will have tight green buds), cut the central head and take out about 8 in/20 cm of stem. Smaller side shoots will develop for a later harvest.

* Brassicas like a slightly higher pH (around 7.5 to 8, which means the soil is more alkaline) than most vegetables favor. You'll have fewer problems with root maggots and clubroot, and they'll thrive. Use horticultural lime to sweeten the soil.

BRICKS

If you are lucky enough to have a brick wall, create interest by removing some of the bricks and filling the holes with soil. Plant small alpine plants, such as *Aubrietia*, in the holes and the plants will cascade down.

* *Thymus pseudolanuginosus*, woolly thyme, loves to be near the warmth of bricks and spreads beautifully.

* Also *Aurinia*, *Iberis*, creeping phlox, *Campanula* and *Sagina* or Irish moss.

BUCKWHEAT

Buckwheat is a wonderful cover crop to bump up poor soil. It adds calcium and keeps weeds away. Once dug under, it acts as green manure. Check farmers' supplies stores for seeds.

BUG JUICE SPRAY

This is revolting but it works. Perhaps the smell of the death of your own species is repellent. Seems logical when you think about it. Try the following: tomato hornworm, cabbage looper, Mexican bean beetle, Japanese beetle, Colorado potato beetle. Gather at least 1 cup/250 mL of the pest and grind them up in an old blender (I could not put them into anything I'd ever use for food again); strain, and add enough water to make a spray. Use on all the plants they attack.

Bug Repellent

There are lots of commercial bug repellents, but the following is ecologically sound and will mess up the leaf-eating pests that drive most of us crazy:

¾ cup/175 mL each	fresh mint leaves
	green onion tops
	horseradish root and leaves
	hot red peppers
2 qt + 1 cup/2 L + 250 mL	water
2 tsp/10 mL	liquid non-detergent soap

Combine first four ingredients in food processor with 1 cup/250 mL water. In bowl, combine the purée and 2 qt/2 L water; strain, stir in soap. Store in fridge. Makes 2 qt/2 L concentrate, which is enough for 2 gal/ 8 L of spray. Add 1 cup/250 mL concentrate to 1 qt/1 L water for spray.

BUG SPRAY, ALL-PURPOSE

Here is a really good deterrent against disease spores. I picked it up in one of my favorite gardening magazines

> 8 jalapeño peppers
> 8 cloves garlic
> 1 qt/1 L water

Blend ingredients in food processor. Dilute 1 part mixture with 4 parts water and spray on plants.

BULBS

I'm a relentless deadheader. Snip off just the tops of tulips and narcissi before they exhaust themselves making new seeds. Leave the plant's foliage to ripen (turn a nasty brown) for next year's food. Once they are yellowed, gently pull out the stalks and toss them into the compost.

* If, like me, you are plagued by animals who eat anything—including the stuff that's supposed to be poison to them (my squirrels dig up the narcissus and fling them about)—try the following: plant tulips and other tasty morsels with recycled plastic berry baskets inverted over them. Flag them so you'll be able to find them easily enough if you want to move the bulbs around.

* This suggestion from a very organized hortbuddy. She uses a variety of mesh boxes depending on the size and number of bulbs to be used—from the small raspberry or cherry tomato boxes right up to the large ones that kiwifruit come in. She places the basket in the hole in the ground and plants the bulbs right in the basket; roots get through the holes easily without damage to them. In fall, the baskets make it easy to take up tender bulbs such as gladioli and dahlias. And for bulbs that stay in the ground (tulips, daffodils and so on), the baskets keep them in clumps by color and size. Attach a plastic stick to each basket with type and color written in permanent marker, so if you want to

move them, at least you know what colors you are carting about even when they aren't in bloom. It's terribly difficult to remember what these bulbs looked like once they are out of bloom. Which explains why I have some truly hideous combinations that continue year after year. This method is also great for finding all the little babies that eventually develop.

* Feeding bulbs: In spring, after flowering is over, and again in the fall, spread bone meal over bulb beds. It will break down very slowly and these two applications should last three years providing phosphorus and nitrogen. If you add blood meal, it will give the plants an immediate hit of nitrogen.

* The main problem with bulbs is the mess they leave behind. Lift them to an out-of-the-way place and replant in fall. I move masses of tulips to a border in the Jardin des Refusés meant strictly for cutting or serious mistakes in color choices, and it's the closest to a riot of color I ever get in the garden.

* Interplant the following to cover up ugly messes and eventually the holes they leave behind: any

veronica; *Galium odoratum*, sweet woodruff; *Brunnera macrophylla*; *Geranium macrorrhizum*; any ferns you can find, especially *Adiantum pedatum*, maidenhair fern; or *Polystichum acrostichoides*, Christmas fern, an evergreen.

* An even better trick is to plant bulbs around flowering shrubs. When the bulbs have finished, the shrubs will be ready to come out and cover up the fading foliage. Peonies are my favorite. The bulbs look wonderful with the young, very beautiful, emergent shoots. The foliage droops in a most salubrious way.

* If you have the time and are a neat freak, this is one method a hortbuddy swears by: braid the leaves once they've finished blooming. It cleans up the mess without robbing the plant of the nutrition it needs to store up for next year's blooms. I have actually seen a whole garden neatened up this way, and it looks really handsome. I do not have the patience.

* Tulip bulbs have a flat side, and if you plant this facing outwards, the largest leaf will face in that direction.

* When planting tulip bulbs for forcing, it works very nicely to place tulips with the flat side of the bulb facing out—that way the large leaf that develops from the flat side will fall gracefully over the side of the pot.

* Feed your spring bulbs in the fall, and after they've finished flowering.

* If you can't figure out which way is up on crocuses, plant them on their sides; they'll grow upward from this position, but won't if they are planted upside down.

* Don't arrange narcissus in a tall, deep vase filled to the brim—they like small quantities of water (about 1 in/2.5 cm).

BURLAP-WRAPPED SHRUBS

Shrubs with rootballs wrapped in burlap can be planted later in the growing season than bareroot plants. Never let bits of burlap show above the soil when planting—they act as wicks, drowning or drying out the roots below. The burlap will eventually break down and won't be harmful to the root system. Even so, I usually get rid of it.

* During the first three or four winters before ericaceous plants, such as rhododendrons, become acclimatized, protect them with a burlap tent. These tents are not beautiful, but might save an expensive plant. Make sure the stakes are driven in a few feet away from the outside edge of the plant—be absolutely sure you aren't hitting any of the shallow and tender roots. Staple the burlap to the stakes.

* Any plant whose roots have been double-wrapped in burlap is a poor bet. That means it's been in the nursery and out of the field so long that it's had to be wrapped a second time.

Cabbage Fly

Twist foil around the roots of a young cabbage plant to fend off the larvae of the cabbage fly.

Cabbage Moth

Plant sage with cabbage and broccoli to repel both cabbage moths and cabbage looper.

Cabbage Worms

Pick a large tough bottom leaf and put it on top of the plant. It will attract the worms and you can easily get rid of both leaf and worms.

Cabbages

Members of the brassica family deplete the soil of nitrogen; therefore, they need a four-year rotation cycle. The flowering members, broccoli and cauliflower, require phosphorus and high levels of calcium, which become major nutrients in their leaves.

* Grow cabbages in white clover. Shear back the clover for a nitrogen-rich mulch.

* Mulching with rhubarb leaves, which contain oxalic acid, helps prevent clubroot disease in the brassica family. Clubroot disease can also be treated with generous amounts of lime.

* Leave six to eight bottom leaves on the root when you cut off the head. The tiny new heads that form are real delicacies.

* By planting dill close, but not too close, to cabbages, cabbage moths will become confused, aphids will be attracted to the plants away from the cabbages. Aphids will bring on more predators against the moths.

* Sprinkle rye flour over cabbage plants to catch cabbage worms and moths and dry them out.

CACTUS

Some people get as hooked on cacti as I do on other plants.
* To get a cactus to bloom, water sparingly—once a month or so—and leave outside in a dry sunny spot as late as possible in the fall—make sure you bring it indoors when temperatures really drop at night. Freezing daytime temperatures along with the drought you're providing should stimulate blooming the following spring.

Calcium

You know you have poor soil when sheep sorrel grows readily or a green scum forms on the surface. Plant lupines to add calcium to the soil.

* Put melon leaves in the compost for an additional hit of calcium.

Carrot Rust Fly

To deter the carrot rust fly, which produces maggoty, deformed carrots, don't plant in the same area year after year. Rotate crops until the maggots die of starvation.

* Interplant carrots with parsley, leeks, onions and sage to help eliminate the carrot rust fly larvae. Pull them out by hand, and till the soil deeply to reduce any overwintering population.

* Interplant carrots, onions and leeks to decrease the

possibility of carrot and onion rust fly—they will be completely confused by the different smells.

* Mix used tea leaves into the carrot seed before planting.
* This fly attacks celery, parsnips, parsley, dill and Queen Anne's lace, so avoid planting them in infested areas.
* Make an infusion of wormwood and pour it around plants in the fall. (See *Artemisia absinthium*.) Plant leeks and sage nearby. Or sprinkle Bacillus thuringiensis (Bt) around these vegetables to get rid of the worm. Plant early under row covers to keep the adult fly from laying eggs.
* Stir crumbled mothballs into the soil to protect the plants against the larvae.

Carrots

When I do radio talk shows during the growing season, the questions that come up most often are about the simple carrot. Carrots seem to give people more than the usual number of problems.

* Carrots are in the parsley family, *Umbelliferae*, as are coriander, dill, fennel and Queen Anne's lace.

* Carrots have really great long taproots that need deep, deep digging to at least 1 ft/30 cm, and lots of compost or composted manure added to the top of the soil. In addition, they like plenty of potassium and phosphorus.

* If you plant a second crop in June, you'll have carrots right up to frost. (A touch of frost makes them sweeter.)

* Put in a few Queen Anne's lace and let the serious munchers—butterflies and caterpillars—feed on them instead of your precious crop.

* Don't plant dill near carrots. It is said to suppress carrot growth.

* In clay soil, plant carrots in trenches filled with soil that's been amended with manure or compost. A good size trench for a garden is 10 ft/3 m long by 1 ft/30 cm wide and deep. Mix equal parts compost, sand

and wet peat moss with approximately 2 cups/500 mL of bone meal and an equal amount of wood ash for phosphorus, potash and trace elements. Rake the site level, water and plant.

* Carrots need lime, potash and lots of humus but not too much nitrogen.
* Carrots need full sun. Hill up soil over exposed carrot tops to prevent green shoulders.
* Carrots and peas make good companions.
* Winter carrot crop: Plant seeds in a cold frame in August and close the frame when frost hits. In November, add compost to the soil; in December, fill the frame with straw. Harvest during winter. Replant during the growing season whenever you pull carrots.

CASTOR BEAN *Ricinus communis*

All parts of this exotic-looking plant are poisonous, but it does help repel such disparate pests as mosquitoes and moles. Plant every 6 ft/2 m as an effective barrier around a vegetable garden. They are easy to grow from seed.

* In garden design they give a lush, almost jungle-like, quality to a bright corner. This annual can grow to 15 ft/4.5 m. Try some of the more interesting varieties, such as 'Borboniensis arboreus', which has red stems and a blue-gray leaf.

Cat Litter

Cat litter is now being made with recycled newspapers and can be recycled yet one more time. Remove the feces (dig a deep hole in an out-of-the-way place and put them there), then dump used cat litter into the compost. It will lighten things up.

* Use cat litter as an excellent ecological substitute for salt to make sidewalks safe to walk on. It will attract warmth and melt ice, or roughen the surface if it's added early enough.

CATMINT *Nepeta mussinii*

Catmint comes in many forms, from small to large, and it is a stunning edger. It needs a fair amount of sun, which I can't provide, but even though it flops about, the intense blue flowers are a real treat.

* If leggy, whack it back to get a flush of new growth and rebloom.

CATNIP *Nepeta cataria*

Don't confuse this plant with the ornamental *Nepeta mussinii*, catmint. Catnip has a natural insect repellent in it. Steep the fresh herb in water and sprinkle the infusion around plants. It will drive off flea beetles. When catnip is freshly picked, it keeps ants from cupboards. (Of course, your cat may have other ideas about what to do with the catnip—mine was a real junkie.)

* If you want to keep cats out of specific areas of your

garden, put a catnip plant in another area where you don't mind them. However, just about every cat in the neighborhood will come for a little roll.

* The pungent scent of catnip should repel aphids, Japanese beetles, squash bugs and weevils from specific plants. And it attracts bees.

Cats

Even for a maven like me, cats can be a royal pain in the garden. My cat Mickie used to plunk her rather large carcass right in the middle of a treasured heath that was almost as old as she was (she died at 18, we think). To discourage Mick, early in the season I'd put sharp pointed sticks in the ground to protrude through the crown as the plant grows. The occasional bit of thorny rose stem dropped around other defenseless plants also kept her away.

* Another way to discourage cats from messing about with plants is to grind up grapefruit and lemon rind

in the food processor and spread the mixture over the soil after planting. This also protects seedlings and adds a little acid to the soil.

Celery

Celery definitely needs companions for a good harvest. Leeks are by far the best. It does well in the shade of beans and tomatoes.

* Celery benefits brassicas by deterring cabbage and white butterflies. If left to flower, celery and leeks attract lots of beneficial insects, especially predatory wasps.
* Celery likes potash. A good source is wood ash saved from wood stoves and fireplaces.

Children in the Garden

After raising four children and not one a gardener, I'm counting on the next generation to be my soul mates. If you want to welcome children into the garden, prepare a special place for them that is their own—located so that they can be seen, for safety's sake, but where they will feel cossetted and private. A small barrier of low plants will do a satisfactory job.

* Provide sure-fire seeds that they can plant wherever they want in their own area. No interference or imposition of adult aesthetics: scarlet runner beans and everbearing strawberry plants are much more fun than the usual radishes (I don't know a kid who loves to eat radishes), and sunflowers, the bigger and grosser the better.

* Build a raised platform to act as a clubhouse or boat or whatever their fantasy life will turn it into.

* Make a special border for children no more than a few feet/meters wide and a few yards/meters long in soil that's easy to work. It's important that they dig into the earth, and learn to love our best friends, worms.

* Plant a cucumber seed and when it's the size of a gherkin put it into a wide-mouthed bottle placed on

its side. Give it shelter so that the plant won't fry. This is weird but kids like it.

* Give them a choice of flowers to attract butterflies, such as nasturtiums and asters. Let kids decide on their own colors—you can be sure they won't be the same as your own.

* Teach them which plants might be poisonous in the garden, such as aconitum, rhubarb, potato vines. (See also POISONOUS PLANTS.)

* And teach them about composting: dig kitchen scraps into their own hole at the edge of the border.

* Personal and sacred totems are always important, whether it's a toy car or a shell. Just keep your hands off, and don't question their choices, even if you find them quirky.

* If you decide to build structures or raised beds where children are playing, don't use pressure-treated wood. The wood is treated with enough arsenic to affect the soil around it. Cedar is better. If you are worried about preserving wood, use a borax-based preservative which is not toxic to humans.

* Here is a wood preservative I found in *COGnition* (the newsletter of the Canadian Organic Growers):

3 cups/750 mL	exterior varnish OR
1½ cups/375 mL	boiled linseed oil
1 oz/25 g	paraffin wax
	Enough solvent (mineral spirits, paint thinner or turpentine) at room temperature to make up a gallon of the mix.

Melt the paraffin in a double boiler. Away from the heat, stir solvent vigorously; slowly stir in the paraffin. Add the varnish or linseed oil while stirring thoroughly.

CHIVES *Allium schoenoprasum*

Chives are alliums, part of the onion family. We take chives for granted and forget that they are not only good to eat but also ornamental. The flowers are tasty when young—a decorative condiment in cold soups. Pick just as the buds begin to form.

* Grow next to gooseberries to keep mildew away.

* Use as a spray to combat downy and powdery mildew.

* Plant to discourage aphids on chrysanthemums, sunflowers and tomatoes.

* *A. tuberosum*, garlic chive, stands straight up, makes a good clump, is long lasting, attracts bees madly and is a gorgeous cut flower. It's the easiest thing in the world to grow and has the added benefit of being good in salads. Blooms in late summer to early fall. Of course, there is a caveat to all these great virtues: it seeds unbelievably. Let it get away from you and you'll have enough to start a garlic chive farm. Every three years divide up the clump. And keep deadheading.

CHLOROSIS

When you see a plant with its veins showing or yellowing, it has a form of chlorosis, which means some mineral is missing. It could be iron, which is needed for plant growth and has become unavailable to the plant. Plants under stress, over-fertilized or in compacted soil can become affected.

*Dissolve a tablespoon of Epsom Salts in a quart of water and spray it on the foliage; or take a handful and sprinkle it around the base at the drip line.

CHRISTMAS TREES

Here's a great way to use all your recycling skills. Stick evergreen branches into huge pots as outdoor bouquets. Add a few more from bright red shrubs such as *Cornus alba* 'Sibirica', dogwood, and you have a stunning display. Of course, they are the best mulch for acid-loving plants. If you tie branches to a fence and add suet and fruit, the birds will love you.

Citrus Fruits

Citrus skins tend to stink up the compost and take forever to break down, but don't throw them out. Orange and grapefruit skins have a number of uses in the garden. They help get rid of radish and onion maggots. Ground up, they add acid to the soil.

* Citrus seeds, especially grapefruit, contain limonin, an oily substance that interrupts the breeding cycle of Colorado potato beetles, Mexican bean beetles, corn ear worms and fall army worms, all of which attack vegetables.

* Let ½ cup/125 mL seeds dry over several days. Crush in a grinder. Let the oily mash dry for a week. Mix the paste with 4 qt/4 L of water to make a spray.

CLAY POTS

I have a small, interesting collection of old and new clay pots. In our climate, with its heavy-duty freeze-thaw cycles, they can't stay outdoors all winter or they shatter. Here's what I do to keep them looking good:

* When much white stuff has collected on the outside of the pots, I disinfect them by immersing them in boiling water or heating them briefly in a 180°F/85°C oven.

* No matter how you clean a clay pot, soak it in water for a few hours before planting—otherwise, it will draw water out of the potting mix.

* To store clay pots, leave them with soil and plants intact. Cut back plants, soak well, and put someplace that's out of the wind and raised off the ground so they won't freeze, or in colder areas, clean them in the fall, turn upside down, place lots of newspaper between each pot and store in a shed or garage.

* If this is not practical, bring pots into the house, clean them up and fill them with dried flowers and grasses.

It's quite cheery, attracts an enormous amount of dust, but gives you some contact with your garden all winter.

CLEANING PLANTS

If you have a Water Pik or any other dental appliance that squirts water, use it to clean insects off plants. A direct hit will kill most soft-bodied indoor pests. Naturally, you'll clean your plants in the shower where you aren't hitting everything nearby.

* Try vacuuming insects off plants such as beans, peppers, tomatoes and strawberries with the wand attachment of your machine. Do this when none of the neighbors can spot you. So embarrassing and noisy.

CLEANUP

There's a fine line between being a good steward and a fussy housekeeper. A real gardener knows when to call it quits. Treating the garden as though it's your living room is fine from a designer point of view but not great when it comes to responsible gardening. Think like a forest—project yourself into the forest and think of all those fallen leaves and natural detritus that turn into lovely humus.

* Get rid of everything in your garden that looks diseased, such as roses touched by black spot or lilac leaves covered in mildew. These are fungi that can live all winter underground.

* Rotting leaves of hostas and other soft-leaved plants should be tossed in the compost.

* Don't remove all the seedheads, don't cut every perennial down to the ground and don't touch plants that can survive without your help. It's amazing how well they do when you leave them alone.

* Obviously, you can't leave piles of junk around; they

attract animals who will burrow into them and munch all winter long on susceptible plants.

Clematis

Clematis are among my favorite vines—up trellises or along fences, growing along the ground or into tall shrubs and trees. Big evergreens, such as blue spruce, or deutzia, which can be dull after flowering, provide a natural trellis. Pick the smaller species such as *C. montana*, *C. orientalis* and those that require little or no pruning. Be sure to provide shade for roots.

Flower	*Prune*
Spring	After flowering
Summer or fall	Early spring
Repeat bloom	Light pruning in fall or
(spring and summer/fall)	early spring

* Here's a handy way to remember which ones to cut back: If it's a hybrid it probably flowers on new wood, so cut back in spring to about 1 ft/30 cm from the ground or to a strong bud growth. Always check the info that comes with your vine and leave a permanent marker on it about pruning.

* If it's a species clematis, leave it alone, and just clean out deadwood or bits that are strangling each other every spring.

* Cut *C. tangutica* and other late bloomers back to within 3 ft/9 m of the ground in late spring.

CLOVER

Clover makes a sensational living mulch—interplant with vegetables or fruit. If it springs up in your lawn, don't worry, it adds nitrogen to the soil. Don't plant near any Ranunculaceae, buttercup family. Watch

buttercups proliferate and you'll see clover disappear.
* Because clover stores nitrogen in its root system, cut
the top off for the compost but leave roots intact to
enrich the soil. It is also a superb cover crop for the
vegetable plant.

CLUBROOT

When planting cabbages, bury a stick of
rhubarb here and there in the bed
to prevent clubroot.

CODLING MOTHS

This major apple pest is pink
and white with a brown
head. The new dormant oil

sprays are good but must be used in very early spring; soapy water or fish oil sprays are recommended by Rodale.

* Make this trap: In a yogurt container, blend 1 tsp/5 mL brewer's yeast, 1 tbsp/15 mL molasses and 1 cup/250 mL water. Hang the container in an apple tree.

COLD AREAS.
See NORTHERN GARDENING

COLD FRAMES

These gizmos can be wonderful if you want to start seeds early. This suggestion is so inventive, it's enchanting:

* Set cold frame near a window. Fill an old crockpot

with water and
place in the cold frame
with a three-prong outdoor
extension cord running
from pot to house.
On cold nights
turn the pot on
high to keep plants
warm; in early spring,
when seeds are set out in flats,
turn the pot on low.

I'm tempted.

Color

Good gardeners are like artists, sensitive to composition, scale and, most importantly, color. Get out color charts if you wish, but looking at paintings will help you become visually literate.

* Use the approach of such illustrious gardeners as Gertrude Jekyll and Vita Sackville-West—take a blossom from one plant and place it next to another to see how well they will live together.

* There are so many tones of white that if you decide you want to create a monogarden, see MONOGARDENING before you start.

* White added to any color combination, especially those on the red side of the color scale, makes that color look more intense. Use white to fulfil this function, or to tone down a drift that is too intensely colored.

* I love to use white or variegated plants in shady spots just to lighten the area. Red in shade turns into dark blobs.

* The cool tones of blue make things appear more distant. Keep this in mind for back walls and borders.

* A hit of scarlet makes green look greener; blue in a sweep of yellow—daffodils, for instance—makes them look more luxurious.

* Flowers usually need a field or background to shine

against. Luscious dark green shrubs are one solution, but I like vines much better myself. Here are a few that are most interesting:

* *Schizophragma hydrangeoides* is a self-supporting vine that blossoms in its first few years. It has a substantial leaf that does look like hydrangea, as do the lace-cap flowers.

* *Hydrangea petiolaris* (syn. *H. anomala*) is another favorite, also a self-clinger with midgreen leaves and glorious blossoms. When it's out of bloom it does a splendid job of being a subtle background.

* Ground covers can be a splendid background for almost any plants: *Hedera* spp., ivy, of course, is so strong it adds a tapestry-like background to any group of plants: *Asarum europaeum*, European ginger, is a shiny low-growing ground cover; *Lysimachia nummularia*, creeping Jenny, is highly invasive, easy to get rid of, and a good way to keep soil in place; *Galium odoratum*, sweet woodruff; *Lamium* in its many forms of silver, or deep blue and green foliage; *Lamiastrum* has a stronger texture and goes well with large-leaved

plants; *Ajuga* comes in pink, dark green and bronze forms and is one of the finest of all ground covers. If you want something small and invasive, consider *Veronica repens*, a creeping form of veronica that has a tiny leaf and lovely blue flowers in spring and spreads anywhere. Don't put it in a rockery.

* Plan what kind of blossoms you want to feature and choose a leaf that will be a complement or contrast. For instance, one striking vine, *Ampelopsis brevipedunculata* 'Elegans', variegated porcelain vine, has heart-shaped mottled leaves. An elegant, simple plant such as *Physostegia virginiana* 'Summer Snow', an obedient plant, with bright white flowers and deep green foliage, makes a beautiful contrast in my garden.

COMFREY

Comfrey leaves contain a significant amount of nitrogen, and since this plant seems to know no shame when it comes to proliferating, keep it chopped back and throw the leaves into the compost. It is a nitrogen-rich mulch either in the bottom of planting holes or chopped up and spread around the garden. Excellent for tomatoes. It contains vitamins C and A and is the only plant that contains B12. The carbon-to-nitrogen ratio is equal to manure.

* I actually like the look of the plant and keep large clumps of it in judicious parts of the garden. Right next to the compost bin, for one. In the shade of a rhododendron, for another—the rhodo did nothing until I planted it near the comfrey. I don't know why, but they work well together.

Companion Planting

Whole books have been written on this subject. Some gardeners swear that companion planting works, others deny its efficacy. The concept of companion planting is based on the assumption that the root systems of different species help each other or that something in the roots discourages or encourages growth or beneficial nematodes. It seems to make sense. My favorites are scattered through the book. One I swear by is growing nasturtiums near any plant that attracts aphids. They prefer the nasturtiums and will flock to their blossoms. It's easy to pick them off, but more likely ladybugs will do the chore for you.

* Nasturtiums are also said to repel beetles that attack cantaloupe.

* Another good thing about companion planting is that one plant can shade the other. For instance, growing peppers among the tomatoes. When delicate pepper skins need protection from summer sun, the

tomato plants will be large enough to do the job. Pumpkins and corn have the same relationship.

* Planting corn with beans and squash is an old Indian technique; the corn stalks provide support for the beans to climb up; the beans put the nitrogen that the corn scooped up back into the soil; squash vines cover the ground and keep out weeds. Looks absolutely beautiful as well, which is another bonus of companion planting: those that tend to help each other also tend to look good together.

* Carrots and peas live together happily. Add onion or sage to keep rust fly infestations off carrots.

* Borage is a great plant to attract bees. It accumulates minerals and therefore is a valuable plant for the compost; grows beautifully (in all senses of the word) with strawberries; and is supposed to repel Japanese beetles and tomato hornworms.

COMPOST

I am a nutter about composting. How any gardener can live without this stuff is a mystery. As well as cleaning up the garden and the kitchen, it does more for the soil than any other amenders—and it's free.

* I usually don't wait until compost is completely finished but spread it around at the three-quarters-finished stage and let it continue the breaking down process as a mulch around the garden.

* Rule 1: Never put any protein in the compost. Don't add bones, grease or anything processed—not even vegetable leftovers that have had a dab of margarine or butter on them. I wash my hands if they've touched protein products before I fool around in the compost. Use vegetable parings, refuse from the fridge (the soggy, wilting stuff is perfect), anything chopped up from the garden. Rule 2: Layer your compost: green (vegetable and garden refuse) and brown (soil, semi-decayed matter, dried leaves). This speeds up the breakdown. Too much green will

smell; too much brown will just sit. Rule 3: Don't let it dry out and turn as often as possible. That's it. Nothing particularly mystifying about it. If you have a two-bin composter, all the better. One side will break down while you fill up the other. I have a homemade version with removable slats, which makes it easy to turn the material over. This is important for a speedy breakdown, because oxygen hastens the decaying process.

* I have a terrific sieve that fits over a bushel basket. When one side of the composter looks like it's got enough good black stuff in it to justify the work, I sieve the material into the basket. I pick out the little red wriggler worms that are crucial to the compost and useless elsewhere in the garden and throw them into the side that's still breaking down. Then I spread the compost around the garden wherever it's needed.

* Keep your compost moist. The usual image is a squeezed-out sponge. The other thing to look for is ants. Ants love a dry compost. Poke holes in the compost to make sure moisture gets all the way through.

* Composters aren't always beautiful, so disguise them by allowing a squash or a tomato plant to grow out of the pile. Plant winter squash seeds in the partly decomposed side and there'll be plenty of room for the sprawling vine.

* Quick compost: Line a large garbage can or dark garbage bag with 3 in/8 cm of soil or damp peat moss. Add kitchen waste and garden wastes (nothing diseased, of course). When almost full, add soil to the top, close and set out in full sun for about three weeks. It'll be ready to use even if it hasn't completely broken down.

* To speed things up even more, chop everything into small pieces before adding.

* Add blood meal or fresh manure to hasten the process.

* Weeds to throw in the compost: Stinging nettles speed up decaying. Dandelions extract iron from the soil and give it back to the compost as it breaks down. Salad burnet adds magnesium; sheep sorrel adds phosphorus; chicory and buttercup add potassium. Thistle contains a bit of copper.

* How to use compost: Compost can be added to the garden anytime during the year. I like the look of not-quite-finished compost as a mulch. It sort of evens up the garden. Spread it as thickly as you can on the top of soil near plants, but without letting it touch the rosettes, stalks or stems of plants—which might encourage rotting. Compost is a wonderful place for slugs and other pests to hide out in, but the benefits from the breaking down of compost far outweigh the pests it might attract. Think of this as an easy way to trap them. See also MULCH.

* Compost accelerators: Add high-nitrogen organic material to the compost to speed up the process. Use blood meal, manure or cottonseed meal. Seaweed compost accelerator:

> 1 gal/4 L   water
> 2 lb/1 kg   dried seaweed

Heat water to 140°F/60°C. Crush or grind seaweed in food processor or by hand. Put seaweed in container and pour the hot water over. Steep overnight. If you use fresh seaweed, heat water to 160–170°F/70–80°C. Makes 1 gal/4 L, which should activate 100 cubic feet/ 3 cubic meters of compost.

* Composting in barrows: Barrows are long mounds of earth you can incorporate into your garden design. In fall, start a compost barrow using 20 parts dry carbon (leaves) to 1 part nitrogen-rich material (grass clippings). Make the mounds no more than 3 ft/1 m wide and 3 in/8 cm high and about the same length as your rows of vegetables. They heat up quickly. Let sit until spring. When decomposition reduces the size to 15 in/40 cm, turn the compost piles into the soil. This will attract earthworms and keep the soil friable and moist.

* Compost in a garbage can: Take a galvanized garbage can and remove the bottom with sheet metal cutters. Paint the can to blend in with its surroundings; bury halfway down into the ground. Toss kitchen wastes into it (no bones or anything with protein in it) all winter. In spring, add soil to cover the

decaying food. Plant annuals on top. The garden will grow all around. In fall, cut back the annuals and use the finished compost in the garden.

* Compost in winter: If the winter is mild I don't mind mushing into the depths of the garden to lug kitchen wastes to the proper composter. I keep bags of leaves nearby for layering and to keep things warm for the worms. This also gives me a chance to appreciate how gorgeous the garden is in winter.

* When things get too cold or I just get lazy about composting, just outside the back door I put a large plastic garbage can with a top that animals can't open. I have soil and leaves in bags stored in the tool shed nearby. To start the process, I throw a bit of completed compost full of red wrigglers in with some food (and hope that they survive the cold), make a little nest in the center and toss the usual kitchen stuff in the garbage can and occasionally add either leaves or soil. By spring, a great deal of this has broken down, and it goes into the main composter to finish off.

* Composting in a cold frame: Unused cold frames can be put to work over the winter. Put kitchen waste in a glass-covered cold frame. Even when the temperature drops, there will be steam rising when sun hits the glass. Once spring arrives, the compost is ready to use.

* Compost tea: This is such a useful homemade product, I wouldn't be without it. It acts as an antifungal spray and can reduce damping off (the scourge of all seedlings). Add 1 part finished compost to 6 parts water and stir. I try to leave this for at least a week; others recommend 3 weeks. Cut in half with water before using.

* The spray also helps prevent blight on tomato and potato plants, anthracnose and powdery mildew on grapes and botrytis blight on beans. This is not a cure for these problems but will help prevent them. Reapply every week.

CONTAINER GARDENING

Containers in the garden increase design flexibility. Containers of any sort can be moved to wherever color is needed; they make a dull deck look glamorous and are indispensable for balconies. I like to move them around the garden as the fancy takes me. A group of santolinas in a lovely pot perks up a boring area; a dense pot of browallias adds a shot of color to a dull shady spot.

* Any container used for permanent plantings must be at least 18 in/45 cm in every direction, to ensure that roots have enough soil to protect them during the winter. Obviously, they have to be constructed of material that will withstand the winter. Terracotta cracks in deep frost.

* Always save the plastic popcorn from packing cases. It's a lightweight material to use for drainage if you are worried about how heavy your pots can get. I usually use gravel because I don't move mine around, so I

don't have to worry about weight. Save six-pack annual containers, turn upside-down over drainage hole.

* When orchestrating containers, think up a color and planting scheme. Try a different theme every year. Once I find something absolutely ravishing I tend to stick with it. Here's one bevy of beauties: Silver, blue and white plants in large pots from the Orient or ornamented clay pots. The pots line the steps going into the garden and become incredibly lush. In the various pots I have *Anthemis cupaniana,* with white flowers, which can take some drought; *Teucrium fruticans,* germander, blue flowers, gray leaves; *Helichrysum angustifolia,* curry plant, silver leaves, wonderful scent when you touch it; and *H. petiolatum,* the best sprawling silver-leaved plant for pots; *Erigeron* for delicacy and airy lightness; browallia, a blue annual; artemisias combine well with almost any plant and they winter over just fine. I can't grow *Cerastium tomentosum,* snow-in-summer, in my garden because it's really too invasive so I've combined it with

Artemisia pontica and *A.* 'Silver Queen' in a container for a permanent planting that needs only the occasional watering, they are all so drought-tolerant.

* Golden bacopa with deep burgundy coleus, phormium with a limey yellow potato vine.

* Hostas are perfect pot plants and I use large and small ones both in the garden and on the deck.

* Another of my favorites is pots of ornamental grasses. This is one way to force them into performing the very first year, and then they can be planted out into the garden. *Ophiopogon nigrescens* is a black grass that looks stunning with golden creeping Jenny, *Lysimachia nummularia* 'Aurea'. I made the mistake of putting it in terra cotta and that was too, too dull. *Liriope muscari*, a grass-like plant, has so many forms it's a shame not to try to get each one: a variegated yellow and cream with a deep blue flower that is startling and architectural; a blue and white leaf with blue flower; and the ordinary one, which spreads like crazy in the right spot, works well in a container. The

smaller fescues, which have a wispy blue sheen to them, are always great to try.

* For permanent balcony container gardens, seriously consider putting in some of the larger, more dramatic grasses such as *Miscanthus sinensis* 'Morning Light'; or *Pennisetum setaceum rubrum*, with its delicate red thin leaves. In order to see their real beauty place them so that light can shine through the plants.

* Feed containers with a very mild (about half) solution of seaweed fertilizer every few weeks until the end of August.

Coriander
Coriandrum sativum

Coriander, or cilantro as it's becoming better known, repels aphids. It helps anise to germinate but holds back fennel. I love the distinctive flavor of this refreshing culinary herb. It contains more carotene than parsley and has calcium, protein, minerals, riboflavin, vitamin B₁ and niacin. It's the best thing in the world to perk up ordinary chili sauce or any commercial salsa.

CORMS

Corms and bulbs of tender plants can be stored over the winter in old pantyhose or in the nylon net bags from onions.

* Or fill a paper bag with sand or vermiculite, or use well-moistened peat or perlite. It's important that corms don't dry out. Add a bit of water occasionally, not enough to start growth but enough to keep them from sprouting.

* Dahlias should be stored above 45°F/7°C.

CORN

Though corn is a great vegetable, it uses up incredible amounts of nitrogen from the soil, which must be replaced, preferably by organic methods.

* Never plant tomatoes and corn together; they both attract worms that look alike.

* Companion planting with sunflowers is said to increase yield.

* Keeping animals away is another matter—see RACCOONS and SQUIRRELS for some help.

* Use clover and other high-nitrogen plants as green manure between the rows of corn.

* A cover crop of mixed clover and oats before planting will lessen the chance of white grub infestation.

* Crop rotation benefits corn.

COUCH GRASS

Attacked by a bad infestation of this weed? Then sow turnip seeds thickly around them. The turnips will choke out the grass. This would not be practical or esthetic in the front lawn of course.

COVER CROP

A cover crop, like green manure or living mulches, is a planting that improves the health of the soil and consequently benefits the plants you grow. Though it is not always possible in a small city garden, if you have space in your vegetable patch you'll end up with much healthier fruits and vegetables.

* Soybeans, oats and millet add large quantities of organic matter to the soil. Use them as a winter blanket by sowing in the fall. Hairy vetch and winter rye are a good combination—rye sprouts and grows

quickly; vetch adds nitrogen and attracts beneficial bugs. Plough it under in the spring to add humus.

* Cover crops are a really clever way of reducing weed families and insect infestation (up to 50 percent, it's claimed). They add valuable moisture and organic content to the soil and, in the case of clover, additional nitrogen.

* Cover crops include barley, buckwheat, clover (yellow sweet, red and white), hairy vetch and winter wheat.

CUCUMBERS

Plant cucumbers with corn to keep raccoons away. Apparently, ants don't like them either.

* Sow radish seeds in cucumber hills to protect them from cucumber beetles.

* Plant beans with cucumber to help repel cucumber beetles.

* Drive off bad nematodes by boiling ½ cup/125 mL

sugar in 2 cups/500 mL water. When cool, dilute with 1 gal/4 L water. It dries out the nematodes and attracts bees.

CUT FLOWERS

Always remove the lower leaves from the stems. Don't crush the stems as is so often recommended—that only makes more of a surface for bacteria to attack and cause rot. Use a clean sharp knife, clip off all the lower leaves, then cut at an angle under water and get them straight into your container. Keep changing the water.

* Cut flowers last longer if foxgloves are included in the arrangement. Or make an infusion of foxglove leaves and add it to the water.

* For delphiniums and larkspur, add a bit of sugar to the water.

* For narcissus, add charcoal. But remember the sap will inhibit the longevity of other plants.

* Try this homemade preservative to give cut flowers

a longer life. It's both a mild fungicide and a source of food.

    2 tbsp/25 mL fresh lemon juice
    1 tbsp/15mL sugar
    1½ tsp/7 mL bleach
      1 qt/1 L water

Mix ingredients; add ½ cup to a container of cut flowers.

CUTTINGS

Cuttings of plants can increase your stock.

* Soft cuttings are usually taken after flowering is over, when there is new green growth. The life force is strongest at this stage of a plant's development.
* Hard wood cuttings root best from old wood.
* Other plants grow best when taken from year-old growth.

* Dip cuttings into rooting hormone and then plant in potting soil mix. Keep watered until new root growth appears. A gentle tug will tell you if it's taken or not. Don't do any transplanting until you have new growth.

Cutworm

These are nasty gray or brown caterpillars 1 to 2 in/2.5 to 5 cm long that munch away at night. The adult is a night-flying moth. They can overwinter, and you've got to be on the alert in spring.

* Mulch vulnerable plants with oak leaves to drive cutworms away.

* Recycle those paper towel or toilet paper rolls in the battle against cutworms: Take a section 5 in/13 cm

long, place around each tomato seedling, push about 2 in/5 cm into the earth.

* Or attach a twist tie to a long nail and push the nail partly into the earth so the twist tie can circle the stem and cutworms can't.

* Bacillus thuringiensis (Bt) dusted on seedlings helps protect them. Or sprinkle a bit of cornmeal or bran meal around the plant; the cutworm eats this stuff and explodes.

Dahlias

If dahlias are planted too close to a heat-reflecting wall, the flowers will be small; give them space to breathe.

* Dahlia tubers: If you have lots of dahlia tubers to store, dig a trench about 1 ft/30 cm deep and the same width against a south-facing wall or fence. Fill the trench with leaves and pack them down. Dig up the tubers from the garden; shake off the soil and any moisture clinging to cut stems. Make sure you label them properly by marking each color and variety. (I've dumped a bunch together sure that I wouldn't forget which was which the following spring—nada, totally forgot.) Lay dahlias on top of packed leaves, right side up. Heap more leaves on top to about 3 ft/ 1 m above the ground. To windproof, cover with a piece of chicken wire, but don't pack down the topping

of leaves. And don't cover with a tarp or plastic. Rain and snow will push the leaves down so they are insulated. In spring, remove the tubers and throw the leaves on the compost. Tubers will be covered with sprouts.

Damping Off

This is a dangerous fungus that can hit susceptible seedlings. To inoculate the soil, drench it with a garlic infusion before sowing the seed:

> 1 clove garlic
> 2 cups/500 mL water

Purée garlic with mortar and pestle or put through garlic press. Mix garlic and water in blender. Steep 24 hours; strain. Use as a soil drench or spray on germinating seeds.

* Another drench:

> 2 handfuls fresh chamomile flowers
> (or 2 tbsp/25 mL dried)
> 4 cups/1 L boiling water

Place flowers in pan, pour boiling water over, and steep for 24 hours.

* Cover the soil of the seedling flat with a thin layer of milled sphagnum moss. The bacteria that live in the sphagnum moss produce chemicals that prevent damping off; but make sure the soil has been sterilized.

DANDELION

I always like to have a few of these in the garden because they root so deeply in the soil. Earthworms follow the paths they make into the lower depths. But they exude ethylene gas, inhibiting the growth of plants around them.

* Dandelions bring nutrients to the surface. Keep them cut so they don't produce flowers.
* Wash the newly sprouted leaves and cook like spinach—add to an omelet.
* Pick the sepals from the bottom of the flower and scatter in salads.

DAYLILIES

It's easy to become a collector of these plants if you have the space. Even a small garden will take dozens. They combine well with bulbs because they cover up the detritus left behind in the ripening process. To keep them neat, deadhead every day; seeds won't form and the plant will be that much stronger; after flowering cut the scapes (stems) back to the ground.
* Daylilies can be eaten; the roots are used in Oriental cooking.

DEADHEADING

Deadheading is one of the great pleasures of gardening. To go out each day and snip off dead and dying blooms brings you closer to your plants than almost any other chore. In most cases careful deadheading will result in plants blooming for a second time before setting seed. Cut back to the node closest to the dead blossom.

* One hortbuddy deadheads with other things in mind. She takes two plastic ice cream pails with tight lids into the garden. One contains drying crystals (available from craft stores), the other, layers of paper towels. In the crystal-filled pail she puts flowers for drying; in the other she gathers aromatic blooms such as roses. In no time, she has flowers for wreaths and bouquets in one, and material for potpourri in the other.

* When deadheading, don't leave flower stalks sticking out.

* Cut back to an axil for neatness.

DECIDUOUS TREES

Fall is the ideal time to get woody plants into the ground. The soil is still warm and holds oxygen that will encourage root growth. Plant about six weeks before a killing frost.

* Transplant bareroot or balled-and-burlapped trees when in dormancy. Container-grown plants are best transplanted in fall, but they won't suffer unduly at other times because their root systems are intact.

* Frost and leaf drop are both stress periods for trees. Don't touch them at this time.

* Roots do not mirror the structure of a tree; roots go way beyond the tip of the dripline, often three times the distance. There are feeder roots that run from 3 to 6 in/8 to 15 cm just below the surface. Roots prefer to stay in that top bit of humus. Keep this in mind when you dig holes to plant. The old idea of a deep hole filled with goodies is now replaced by the concept of a hole the depth of the root system and about five times the width. Don't amend the soil. The plant should get

adjusted to its new environment as quickly as possible. Top dress with compost and manure or add leaf mold from the same species of plant. Bacteria that will help it grow are probably present in the leaves.

* Maple, birch and other trees that leaf out early should not be pruned until sap flow starts slowing down—usually in late summer.

* If you want to keep marauding mice and other little animals from chewing on the bark of trees, keep the snow around the trunk packed down.

* Once the ground is frozen, make sure that you move any mulch away from the trunks of trees where small animals, such as mice, may take up nesting for the winter.

* To prevent bark from splitting during winter freeze-thaw cycles, paint the bark with white latex paint watered down by half.

DECK AND PATIO ORGANIZATION

Every year I work away at my deck trying to keep it neat and, at the same time, filled with lots of plants. Patios create the same problem. Get too much stuff on either and they become cramped and messy. Here are some useful tips:

* Add a mirror to give the illusion of depth.

* Always keep the furniture in scale with the size of the deck or patio. One oversized piece is enough in a small space.

* To maximize a fairly small space: Display a whole collection of pots filled with plants on a copy of a Victorian pie cooler—a decorative metal bookshelf that can be folded up and brought indoors in winter.

* A light metal plant holder supports a pot of trailing plants in summer and a large glass ball in winter.

* Old patio furniture tends to be very tough. Cover an old round table with a new slightly larger black painted wooden top and it will look just fine. Paint out the legs with black enamel paint.

* Line steps with huge pots of plants. This gives any area a cossetted feeling and makes a grand entrance.

DEER

Deer can leap fences with great bounds and nibble away at the most succulent of roses without rousing anyone from a good night's sleep.

* The best remedy I've heard of is from a hortguru on the West Coast. She sticks bars of Dial soap (it works better than the other deodorant soaps, she says) in old pantyhose and hangs them about the periphery of her very large country garden.

* Or wrap human, dog or cat hair in old pantyhose and put them in plastic bottles with holes punched in the bottom. (This way, you won't have to replace them when it rains.)

* Organic Gardening suggests getting a few male friends to pee around the perimeter of the garden to mark the territory.

* Get Zoo Poo, scat from major cats works the same way. Both must be renewed after it rains.

* Scatter blood meal around the garden if you don't have a dog (which will more than likely go crazy with pleasure at the smell of blood meal and dig it up).

* I've seen hedges all over the country eaten up to deer height, creating a very curious effect and reducing the hardiness of the hedge. Collect the plastic rings that hold six-packs of beer or pop from recycling bins and connect them with twist ties to form a net. In autumn, attach this uncomfortable netting with twine along the area that attracts the deer. Air and light will get through, but the nibblers won't.

* Use a mash of garlic to keep the deer away from favorite plants (theirs and yours).

Design, New Beds

To see the shape of a bed, lay out a track of flour, sand or lime to indicate the edge. Do this on a calm day.

Check the effect from every window in the house and make
adjustments to keep everything in scale.
* Work out a color scheme,
keeping in mind that flowers bloom, on average,
about three weeks and
what's left is foliage. The
obvious place for foliage
fanatics like me to
begin is with what's
going to be around the
longest. I usually start with shrubs. A silver-gray one
here, something tart and acid yellow there, perhaps a
bit of variegation for the darker end of the bed. This is
called anchoring the bed. Gertrude Jekyll used to use
yuccas to do this; I like certain cotoneasters such as
Cotoneaster dielsianus 'Major', a fountain-shaped
plant with gray leaves, small white flowers and dark
red berries—a four-season beauty; *Amelanchier*

canadensis, serviceberry or *Enkianthus campanulatus*, tall, rather stark and elegant, with really good form. And for something statuesque I might try *Crambe cordifolia*, which has huge leaves and a shower of bright sparkly flowers.

* Don't put all the architectural plants at the back. Mix them up-front and center, at the ends and in the middle: tall ornamental grasses; *Rodgersias; Angelica gigas; Eupatorium spp.*

* Have waves of plants so that the eye is constantly stopped by something surprising, such as a shift in height and density. The effect is looking at plants through plants, almost like an opaque screen. This sensual, veil-like approach to the use of foliage plants draws the eye into the garden and when everything is in bloom provides lots of surprises.

* For a formal effect, edge the beds with santolina, boxwood or yew.

* For a more casual look, soften the edges of beds with plants that like to flop over, such as lavenders;

catmints (a great combination, by the way); *Alchemilla mollis*, Lady's-mantle; bergenia; or some of the smaller ornamental grasses such as *Festuca ovina glauca*, blue sheep's fescue.

DIATOMACEOUS EARTH

This is an organic fertilizer as well as insecticide. It's a powder that's almost pure silica, made from the bodies of ancient sea animals. The edges of the dust are so sharply pointed that small animals such as slugs perish when exposed to the stuff. Alas, it also kills earthworms and birds. Use as a last resort, after a rain (or a slight misting with a water bottle). It contains trace minerals in a chelated (readily available) form. Once washed into the soil, it's really effective.

DISEASE

We spread diseases around mainly by sloppy gardening techniques. That's why it's wise to get anything that has disease or signs of disease right out of the garden as soon as you spot it. For instance, never put rose leaves or any other plant that's susceptible to mildew, such as phlox or Dame's rocket, in the compost. Compost doesn't reach a temperature high enough to destroy black spot or powdery mildew.

* Always keep your equipment clean. This is a pain in the neck, but it really takes only a few minutes at the end of the day to wipe off secateurs and trowels with a little household bleach and rub them with vegetable oil.

* If you are working with diseased material, be sure to wash both your hands and gloves after a session.

DOGS

Dog owners have allowed their little (and big) darlings

to use my garden as their bathroom of choice. Since there are no bad dogs, just thoughtless owners, I devised the following: One woman insisted on letting her dog run into my front garden. After the third time I caught the little mucker digging up my precious plants and yelled at both of them, I told her that I was having the whole place sprayed with a lethal poison to get rid of weeds (something I'd never do, but she didn't know that), that if the dog licked his paws after the treatment he'd become deathly ill and that it was being done the next day. The dog was always on a lead after that and he was kept well away from the garden.

* Epsom Salts sprinkled around edging plants helps keep them away.

* Uncomfortable stones placed judiciously around keep dogs from using a garden as a burial ground for bones.

* Stop them in their tracks by putting a rotten potato in their favorite watering spots. It should be replaced every few weeks.

* If you are an avid gardener but feel the need of a dog, be warned, the following breeds have a genetic

need to dig: all terriers, dachshunds, Siberian huskies. You might want to avoid these. Most dogs will dig if they get bored or there's no one around to play with. If you have a digger, spread some cayenne pepper or citronella in their favorite spots.

* If a dog digs, throw a can filled with sealed-in pea gravel toward it and holler "Stop!" Eventually you'll get your point across.

* Invisible Fencing brand "Pet Containment System" is a possibility. The garden is wired with an antenna buried 2 in/5 cm underground. The pet wears a collar that picks up a small static surge whenever it nears a forbidden area. They learn. Eventually.

* If unwelcome deposits are left, collect and put in an attractive container with a note: "I believe this belongs to you."

DOLOMITE

This is limestone rich in magnesium. Sold as agricultural lime, it adds trace mineral magnesium to soil, and neutralizes soil acidity.

DRIED FLOWERS AND HERBS

The art or craft of drying flowers and making bouquets has taken off in the past few years. I've seen compilations of dried grasses, herbs and perennials that are magnificent. I'm no flower arranger but even I can create an attractive arrangement.

* Herbs make beautiful arrangements, and you can dry any herb in your garden.

* If you want to use herbs for cooking, harvest just before the blooms come out. Place bunches of herbs upside down in a large brown paper bag and hang them in a cool, airy place.

* There's also an amazing array of perennials that can be dried.

* This method works with almost any plant you fancy. I was astonished to see how gorgeous peony

blooms look in a group. Don't let them open completely, and cut them with a fairly long stem. This will also encourage next year's growth.

* The traditional plants to use are everlastings such as globe amaranth; *Limonium*, statice or sea lavender; *Armeria*, sea pink or sea thrift; and honesty. But be imaginative; perhaps a whole wreath of sage or long stems of sage in a bouquet.

* A friend made me a wreath of *Artemisia ludoviciana* 'Silver King', a silvery invasive plant. It's worth growing just for picking and drying. It's aromatic and looks very romantic.

* The stronger the color of the flower, the more arresting a contribution it makes to a bouquet. Take the blue of delphiniums, aconitum or thistle; pinks of astilbes, dahlias, salvias, liatris, roses or yarrow. Cut in the morning after the sun has evaporated any dew from the flower. Do this before they are pollinated— they are just fully open. (This will vary with the plant.) Cut a fair whack of stem and trim off the leaves except those just beneath the flowers. Hang upside down in a dark, airy space for a few weeks.

Earwigs

I am ambivalent about these pests. On the one hand, they eat up garden junk, on the other, they will move on to tasty plants, leaving behind chewed-up leaves. I tend to let them be for the former reason. But if you are plagued by them, set out crumpled newspaper in clay pots at night and first thing in the morning dump them into a pail of water with some vegetable oil added to keep them from crawling out.

* Make traps by bundling together three 10 in/25 cm lengths of old garden hose with tape or twist ties. Put them between rows of vegetables and at the base of shrubs at night. Empty them into the bucket of water and oil in the morning.

* Though they may give painful bites, they are good mothers in the insect world.

EDGING

Broken pieces of concrete sidewalk, which almost every homeowner seems to have lurking under the front porch, can be put to good use in raised beds. Use the rough-looking side, which is studded with pebbles, to edge a bed; let plants spill over the sides to soften the edges. You can always pick up this sort of thing in any local renovation—for free.

EELWORM. See NEMATODES

EPSOM SALTS

* Add a cup to the surface of the soil when you make a new bed.
* Give roses and tomatoes a feed of 1 tsp for each foot of height, every two weeks.

* Apply 1 tbsp over the root area every two or three weeks.

* Sprinkle around the areas where raccoons like to hang out. They hate the taste. Add more when it rains. This won't hurt the soil.

* Epsom Salts also make a good foliar spray: 1 tsp to a pint of water will revive leaves in a week.

Erosion Control

To help anchor soil on hillsides, choose plants with penetrating roots—they will help stabilize the area. *Cotoneaster horizontalis*; conifers such as juniper *Juniperus*; *Tsuga*, hemlock; and *Taxus*, yew, will tolerate a little shade; junipers and pines will stand up to hot sun.

* Try some really hardy invasive plants—mints and ground covers such as *Lysimachia nummularia*, creeping Jenny. They have the bonus of a season of flowering beauty.

EUPHORBIA

These are great favorites. *Euphorbia lathyris*, mole plant, discourages moles from coming into the garden. It's also supposed to discourage mice and therefore should be useful near fruit trees.

* There are dozens of new euphorbias. The sap from these plants can cause an allergic reaction so handle carefully.

* *E. martinii* is evergereen and makes an ideal winter plant. Many have attractive acid green cymes.

EVERGREENS

Evergreen shrubs and trees are best pruned by

removing the central leader on the ends of branches after the new growth has completely formed in late spring. This causes new bud development on the surrounding lateral or side shoots that grow the following spring.

* Evergreens don't go into dormancy in fall, so delay transplanting until spring if there's a threat of frost.

* Be sure to water evergreens before the ground freezes in fall, especially when there's a drying wind. Use very cold water so that you don't change the temperature around the root system.

* In spring, remove the dead or brown parts of dwarf evergreens by rubbing them between your well-gloved hands—rose gloves are excellent. You'll find that new growth will probably start up in a few weeks.

* Very few evergreens are able to stand up to all-round shearing with the exception of *Thuja occidentalis*, arborvitae or eastern white cedar; and *Taxus baccata*, English yew. They make good hedges as well.

* Evergreens that add strong winter interest include *Juniperus x media* 'Pfitzeriana', 'Gold Form' or 'Aurea'.

The golden yellow of these hybrids is a good contrast with the blue of *Juniperus scopulorum*, rocky mountain juniper, which has a more upright form. *Picea pungens* 'Montgomery', Montgomery blue spruce, has an elegant pyramidal form and doesn't become a monster like the ubiquitous *Picea pungens*, Colorado blue spruce, which grows to 100 ft/30 m.

See also NORTHERN GARDENING.

FENNEL *Foeniculum vulgare*

Many vegetables and some herbs, such as coriander and wormwood, don't like growing anywhere near this plant. But it's feathery and statuesque; bronze fennel is particularly ornamental, so grow it as a specimen or in its own bed. In the mixed border, it makes a splendid contrast with both flowers and foliage.

FERNS

Plant them as great disguises for the dying foliage left behind by bulbs and for the legginess of old shrubs such as rhodos and azaleas. They are also a handsome transition section from one part of the garden to the next. This is a particularly good solution if you wish to demarcate garden from countryside. Most are forgiving plants and many do well in dry shade.

* Fall is the best time to plant. Make sure you place the crown at the surface level of the soil. Add lots of humus in the form of leaf mold and compost, water, and provide a bit of shade.

* Combine with *Sanguinaria canadensis*, bloodroot; *Cypripedium acaule*, lady's-slipper; and hostas such as *H.* 'Halcyon' or *H.* 'Blue Cadet'.

* *Polystichum acrostichoides*, Christmas fern, will survive most severe winters. It grows from 2 ft/60 cm to 3 ft/1 m.

* Don't forget that some ferns look marvellous in pots: *Athyrium goeringianum* 'Pictum' has fronds of silver, bronze and metallic green.

* Give ferns a mulch of leaves before winter sets in.

FERTILIZER

Fertilizer is anything added that improves the fertility of the soil. A good fertilizer feeds the soil and is the safest way to fertilize a plant. A fertile soil will have a balance of minerals and micronutrients so subtle that no chemical can possibly emulate it. However, the breaking down of manure, compost and leaf mold will.

* Organic fertilizers improve the water retention in soil, fix nitrogen and, most important of all, make nutrients accessible to the plants when they need it.

* One of the essentials for the growth and health of any plant is nitrogen. If leaves start to yellow it usually means there's a nitrogen deficiency. Add compost, manure, blood meal, bone meal, grass clippings and other garden wastes. See NITROGEN.

* Then comes phosphorus, which is crucial to seed development, disease resistance and plant growth. Add phosphate rock powder, bone meal or blood meal. (Add 5 parts manure to 2 parts phosphate.) Mix

manure and phosphate, and then spread around evenly.

* Potassium (potash or potassium oxide) is necessary for early growth and stem strength and is essential to the formation of carbohydrates necessary for protein in the plant. Use manure and compost, minerals such as granite dust and plant litter as well as wood ash. Seaweed helps raise the potash level. See POTASH; POTASSIUM.

* Lightning storms add hundreds of thousands of tons of nitrogen to the soil every day by converting existing nitrogen in the air and making it available instantly in the soil. Rain and snow add nitrogen, as well as phosphorus and trace minerals, which may help explain why crops in the far north grow so well.

* Roses are heavy feeders, so give them lots of food. Here's an organic fertilizer treat for them:

> 2 parts fishmeal
> 2 parts blood meal
> 1 part cottonseed meal

1 part rock phosphate
1 part **greensand (an iron potassium
        silicate or a glauconite potash
        mineral)

Mix in bucket, store in cool dark place. Every month apply 1 to 3 cups/250 to 750 mL to each rose.
For acid soil, add 1 part wood ash.
* Bulbs:

1 part blood meal
1 part bone meal
1 part wood ash

Combine and scatter over bulb beds in fall.
* Alfalfa as fertilizer: Alfalfa has tap roots that fix nitrogen in the soil and draw iron, phosphorus, potassium, magnesium and trace minerals from the subsoil. On a large property, cut and leave for mulch. In a smaller vegetable garden, plant alfalfa between

rows and cut every few weeks in spring; slow down in summer. Once established, it provides a great weed-free mat for garden paths.

* Alfalfa infusion: Soak alfalfa leaves in water for a few days; strain. Pour the water around heavy feeders in the vegetable garden such as broccoli, cauliflower, tomatoes, peppers and corn.

* Comfrey:

>   2 cups/500 mL chopped comfrey leaves
>   4 cups/ 1 L water

Combine in a saucepan, bring to boil. Steep, let cool and strain. The infusion is high in potassium and an excellent foliar fertilizer. Spray on the leaves of tomatoes, peppers, eggplant, okra and berries, just as they begin to set fruit. Seems to help against blossom end rot and fungus diseases, like verticillium and fusarium blight.

* A bulk organic 5–10–10 fertilizer from Rodale:

17 lb/8 kg	**cottonseed meal
8 lb/4 kg	**colloidal phosphate
45 lb/20 kg	granite dust

* "Sam Dunbarr's Fertilizer Tea Barrel" flower and vegetable fertilizer:

	Green plant residue from garden
4 gal/15 L	manure
2 cups/500 mL	fish emulsion
2 cups/500 mL	seaweed extract
½ gal/2 L	blackstrap molasses

Place a heavy screen on top of a brick in the bottom of a 50 gal/190 L barrel so it rests about 1 in/2.5 cm above a spigot inserted in the side. This acts as a filter. Fill the barrel to within 1 ft/30 cm of the rim with plant detritus. Dump manure into a burlap sack and place on top of plant material. Add the next three ingredients. Fill barrel with water and allow to steep several days before drawing off through the spigot. Use this goop undiluted as a soil drench. I don't have the room to set up such an elaborate operation in my own small garden, but it sounds terrific if you've got the space.

* Fish tank fertilizer: Instead of dumping water rich in fish manure down the drain, try it on your rose beds, borders and vegetables. It's free and at the end of the season, switch to putting it on the compost pile.

FLEA BEETLES

Flea beetles prefer full sun and dry conditions, so spatter their favorite plants with water at the height of the day. Place vulnerable plants next to tall ones that will partly shade them. Add compost.

* Place tansy leaves and stems along the row affected or between plants in a raised bed. This will usually send them

elsewhere. Regular weeding, cultivating shallowly around plants and spreading wood ash will help.

* Make the following tea:

    1 cup/250 mL tansy leaves
            6 cloves garlic
   3 cups/750 mL water

Blend ingredients and strain. Spray on susceptible plants.

* An alternative tea can be made from summer savory, wormwood, bindweed and garlic. Blend these ingredients with water and strain.

* Mix various plants to confuse beetles; plant resistant varieties usually with hairy or waxy leaves. Be sure to keep the garden free of weeds and detritus.

* Bruised elderberry leaves laid on plants will help deter them. The beetles are also repelled by mint and wormwood.

Frost

Always keep a record of the frost dates in your own garden rather than in your general area. You can more accurately seed beans, peas, carrots, head lettuce and beets 60 days before the first frost and you'll get a fall harvest. Spinach, leaf lettuce and radishes can be seeded as late as 30 days before first frost. Most plants can be moved around up to the first light frost.

* Deciduous hedges, trees and shrubs can be planted even if there is slight frost in the ground. If you buy plants late in the season when they are on sale, prepare the right size hole in advance, store the soil where it won't freeze and use it for backfilling the hole. But don't plant evergreens, which do not go into dormancy in winter, after first frost. See also EVERGREENS.

* If there's a threat of frost and I haven't brought containers in or there are still tomatoes on the vines, I throw old sheets over them early in the evening. This holds in the heat of the day and generally protects them very well.

* Try to keep from planting in a frost pocket. This could be a depression in the ground or at the bottom of a hill where the heavy cold air can sink like a stone. Frost is more likely to hit here first, or on the windy side of a hedge or copse where cold air builds up against the barrier. See also NORTHERN GARDENING.

FRUIT

Crab apples set the next season's flower buds from mid-June to early July, so prune immediately after blossom time.

* Raspberries grow well in the partial shade of English walnut trees and are one of the plants that grow in natural association with them.

* Blueberries don't ripen off the bush—pick them sour, they stay sour. Leave them alone for several days after they've turned blue to get the best taste. Try to resist harvesting blueberries until the third year after

planting—you'll encourage shoot growth on new plants if you remove blossoms during the first two years.

FRUIT FLIES

These little guys bother people, though they really don't cause any damage. If you have an indoor worm composter or holding pot for the composter, stick a couple of strips of fly paper inside the lid.

* An alkaline environment is less likely to support the growth of yeast (where the fruit flies love to dine). To reduce pH, add lime, calcium carbonate or powdered egg shells to the bin.

* To raise pH, add acidic pine needles, coffee grounds or even ground-up citrus peel.

Fruit Trees

For a healthy orchard, interplant with a combination of 15 percent mustard seed with clovers.
* Plant chives, garlic, onions, nasturtiums, horseradish, southernwood and stinging nettle between rows of trees.
* Grow peanut plants between nut trees.

Fumigation

If you have a greenhouse filled with aphids, ants, termites or whitefly, make a smoke from oak leaves. Let the smoke roil around for about half an hour before ventilating.

Fungal Diseases

The major problem with fungal diseases is that most

of them are systemic. They get into a leaf, the leaf falls to the ground, fungus overwinters, then starts from the ground up, infecting the plant.

* Baking soda, it turns out, is one of your best buys for cleaning the house and equally useful in the garden. Use 2 tbsp/25 mL in 2 qt/2 L water, and spray infected plants.

* For black spot use 5 tbsp/75 mL baking soda in 5 gal/20 L water. Add a few drops of insecticidal soap or mild detergent to help it stick to the target. Spray both top and bottom of leaves.

* Inhibit the spread of fungal diseases by combining clematis leaves, corn leaves and the papery outer garlic leaves. Process this unlikely lot in a blender with enough water to make a slurry; strain, and spray on plants.

* Try commercial anti-dessicants to fight fungal diseases. They are also a good organic spray against powdery mildew on roses, zinnias and lilacs. Apply several times during growing season at half the manufacturer's recommended strength.

* *Equisetum arvense*, horsetail, contains silica, which is excellent for controlling powdery mildew:

> 1 cup/250 mL chopped horsetail
> 1 qt/1 L water

Mix together and boil for 20 minutes. Cool; strain. Spray or apply as a soil drench to prevent damping off.
* Mix 3 tbsp/50 mL household bleach in 1 gal/4 L water. Applied as a soil drench, it may also help get rid of fungi.

GARDEN ORNAMENTS

Garden ornaments will enhance any garden. They add layers of meaning, and, in many cases, can be lots of fun. I use personal totems to adorn my own garden—a shell my father gave me, gears from old farm machinery, a glass fishing ball—small things with an emotional connection. Some are small surprises hidden under a large leaf and seen only in fall or spring.

* When you buy garden furniture, make sure it's in scale with the size of your garden. Huge pieces in small spaces look awkward, just as ditzy little pieces look like an unnecessary frill.

* Look for cast-offs on garbage recycling day. An abandoned fire iron can be a plant prop; an iron grid can grace a fence or hold up vines.

* New pieces of statuary and stone furniture can be made to look old. See AGING; PATINA.

* Place ornaments as subtly as possible—a fleeting glimpse rather than a spotlight.

* Smother them with mosses or vines. And never, ever take them too seriously.

GARLIC *Allium sativum*

This is one of the most useful plants in the garden. Apart from the delight of eating fresh garlic, I plant it beside rose bushes to ward off fungal diseases and throughout the rest of the garden to maintain healthy soil.

* Oil of garlic is a powerful insecticide that kills aphids when used in a spray. Garlic produces enzymes in its bulb that interact with the sulphur produced by microorganisms in humus.

* Because it's a natural fungicide, interplant with cabbages, tomatoes, eggplants and fruit trees.
* Here's a recipe from a wonderful book called *Carrots Love Tomatoes* by Louise Riotte:

> 2–3 oz/50–75 g chopped garlic
> 2 tbsp/25 mL mineral oil
> 1 tsp/5 mL fish emulsion
> 2 cups/500 mL water

Soak garlic bulbs in mineral oil for a day. Dissolve fish emulsion in water; stir into garlic and oil. Strain, and keep the liquid in a glass container. Dilute 1:20 with water and use as a spray against most garden pests. This may discourage rabbits from attacking sweet potatoes.

* Garlic spray controls blight on tomatoes and potatoes.
* To ward off borers, plant garlic around trees.
* Some claim that grated garlic helps many bulbs, tubers and woody plants to break dormancy. Gladiolus

corms treated with garlic paste sprout ten days earlier than untreated corms, according to one experiment.

* Plant garlic in spring for fall harvesting. I plant in the fall to get a good start on next year's crop. Cut back flower stalks to let the bulb develop underground.

* Never keep garlic in the refrigerator. Store in container with holes so it can breathe.

Geraniums Cranesbills

If I had limitless space, I'd plant as many hardy geraniums as I could find. They come in a marvellous variety of colors, from whites, pinks, magentas, blues and purples. Keep them deadheaded and they'll bloom profusely. They seem untouched by diseases and pests, and with some good snipping can make perfect mounds.

* Geraniums for the shade: *Geranium macrorrhizum* has lovely aromatic foliage, boring magenta flowers, I

think, and it will spread into neg-
lected spots. It's a good nurse plant
for keeping weeds at bay and pulls
out easily. *G. m.* 'Ingwersen's Variety'
and *G. m.* 'Album' look right with
ferns, astilbes and hostas in a
woodland setting.

* For semishaded areas:
G. maculatum in white
and pink is particularly
tough and will pop up in
surprising places, including cracks in stone.

* And to cap off your garden: *G.* 'Johnson's Blue'
combined with Asiatic lilies—both grow to 2 ft/60 cm
and bloom at the same time. *G. endressii* is silver-
pink, with funnel-shaped flowers and slight striations
of red. *G. e.* 'Wargrave Pink' is sturdier and combines
well with *Stachys*, lamb's ears and veronicas; *G. san-
guineum* 'Lancastriense'; *G. cinereum* 'Ballerina'; *G.
renardii*; and *G. pratense*.

* *G. renardii* 'Philippe Patel' has strong leaf form;
G. 'Rozanne' blooms all summer.

GERANIUMS *Zonal Pelargoniums*

We call them geraniums but they are in a different
family than the hardy geranium (Cranesbill, above).
These plants are heat lovers from South Africa and,
amazingly, need no fertilization. When bringing
them inside, give them a good dunking in warm
soapy water, which acts as an insecticide.

* For January bloom: Cut roots back to fit into a 6
in/15 cm pot, cut tops back to the same length as the
root and remove all leaves. Wash and dry the pot,
plant the stripped-down geranium in good potting
soil and put it in the sunniest window you have.

* A winter in semi-dormancy: Leave it in its pot, cut
the stem back to 6 in/15 cm and store in a cool, dark
place where the air can circulate. Water every few
weeks but don't soak. Just a top watering will do.

When the first green comes out in midwinter, slowly increase the ration of light.

* A winter in full dormancy: Don't cut the plant back unless it's humongous. Remove from pot and shake off the soil. Hang the plant upside down in any material that allows air circulation. In February, repot the plant, water, and gradually introduce to the light.

* In August, add to your supply by nipping off 2 in/ 5 cm from the tip of the stem at an existing joint. Pull off any leaves and dip the cut end into a rooting medium. Plant in a clean clay pot with good potting soil. Water thoroughly. Put the potted cutting in a clear plastic bag and keep out of direct light for a couple of weeks. When you see new growth, take the pot out of the bag and give it as much light as possible. This method is also effective in February.

* Always introduce to the out of doors slowly, as the weather warms up in spring.

* White geraniums and corn, planted with roses, repel Japanese beetle.

* Look for gold or silver leaf zonals which will tolerate light shade.

GLADIOLAS

Soak corms for two hours in a mix of water and fertilizer (water soluble, of course), then plant. This will give them a good start on life and makes for better growth. Plant them every 10 days until mid-July for a succession of bloom.

GOLDENROD

This poor plant gets a bad rap. It is not a pollen producer like ragweed; it doesn't cause allergenic reactions. The seed of goldenrod is too heavy to waft about on the air. Make sure you cut it down before it goes to seed or you will have a huge crop next year. Add lots of humus to the soil.

GOPHERS

I've only heard about the more violent methods of getting rid of gophers. However, scillas are supposed to keep them out of the garden, and these little bulbs will naturalize everywhere, making an ornamental carpet with their dancing blue flowers.

GRAPEVINES

Grapes prefer slightly acid soil and a humid moist climate with good air circulation. You'll get mildew if you don't have the latter. These vines won't get brown rot or mildew if grown up elm or mulberry trees.

* Hyssop planted with grapes increases the yield. Keep grass away.
* For good fruit production: Prune back 2 or 3 buds the first year. Cut out the branches that fruited this season each fall.

GRASSES, ORNAMENTAL

Every garden can use ornamental grasses somewhere in the border. They move with the wind, give interest from fall through winter, and can't help but add some height and zing to a border design.

* Though it has become the fashion to have borders consisting of nothing but grasses, I prefer to mix them with perennials and small shrubs. They look splendid combined with peonies, broadleaf evergreens and perennials. They are especially effective with the static quality of dwarf evergreens. The colors range from scarlet to deep bronze, variegated yellow to all forms of green.

* When placing grasses make sure they can be seen with the sun streaming through them. Backlighting these plants will show just how graceful and delicate they are.

* They can be planted in the garden almost up to hard frost. The more tender varieties can be potted up and brought indoors for continued pleasure.

* In spring, whack most grasses back to within 3 in/ 7.5 cm from the ground.

* Some grasses are self-cleaning so just leave them alone. If they look untidy in spring, pull out the brown stalks.

* Here are some particularly beautiful forms: *Helictotrichon*, a steely blue; *Molinia caerulea variegata* is a crisp clump; *Carex siderosticha*, a spreader with elegant long green leaves with white margins.

* *Miscanthus sinensis giganticus*, giant eulalie, and *M. s. strictus*, zebra grass, both look great beside swimming pools.

* Plants that keep their color over the winter: *Carex buchananii*, Buchanan's sedge, is a magnificent bronze; *Carex Comans* 'Bronze Form' even more intense hue;

Imperata cylindrica 'Red Baron', Japanese blood grass; *Carex albula*, frosty green carex; and *Uncinia uncinoides*, New Zealand sedge. *Ophiopogon planiscapus* 'Nigrescens' is a black grass that works just as well in containers as it does in the ground, where it will eventually spread.

* Bring gold into the shade with *Hakonechloa macra* 'Aureola'. It flows beautifully from a container as well.
* Use grasses in window boxes for winter interest.

Green Manure

Add vegetable matter to the soil to insulate it, protect it from erosion during the winter and keep it warmer in summer. This will also encourage earthworms, which draw up nutrients from deep within the soil.

* Kale is a good winter green manure. The taste improves with a touch of frost, and it survives beautifully under a blanket of snow. Dig it under in the spring. See also Cover Crops.

HANDS

Use the oldest trick in the book before you go out into the garden to work. Run your fingernails along a bar of soap and then wear gloves. I keep forgetting and am reconciled to the fact that my fingernails will probably be dirty until Christmas.

* Wash filthy hands after a day of gardening with a mix of water and denture plaque remover. It's better than bleach and a lot easier on the skin.

* All gardeners live with rough hands, but they can be rejuvenated by one of the oldest salves around—Bag Balm, a commercial product used to massage the chapped nipples of cows. Crabtree & Evelyn's Hand Recovery works wonders on both hands and feet.

* My favorite gloves are called Foxgloves. They wash up easily and are like a second skin.

HEDGES

Hedges are ideal to form the bones of your garden. They provide a background for plants, give you privacy and cut down noise, whether from nearby roads or the general drone of the city. The calming effect of a hedge can be a major contribution to your garden.

* Here are some excellent hedging plants: *Taxus baccata*, English yew; *Carpinus betulus*, hornbeam; *Thuja plicata*, Western red cedar; *Ligustrum ovalifolium* 'Aureum', golden privet; *Fagus sylvatica*, beech; *Buxus*, box; *B. koreana*, Korean box, tends to be the hardiest; *Ilex*, holly; *Rosa rugosa*.

* Planting guidelines for formal hedges: Dwarf, under 3 ft/1 m, plant 18 in/50 cm apart; up to 7 ft/2 m tall, plant 2 per yard/meter; taller hedges, plant three for every 7 ft/2 m. Be sure to plant at least 2 ft/60 cm inside your property line so you don't trespass on your neighbor's property.

* The easiest way to plant a hedge is to dig a trench 3 ft/ 1 m wide and 2 ft/60 cm deep; run a string down the

center. Place each plant against the string as a guide, fill in with soil and tamp. Water deeply for the first year.

* To prune: Choose the shortest plant, shear everything else off to this height, and trim the sides. Make the bottom of the hedge wider than the top so light can get at the center and snow won't crush it.

* Cut evergreen hedges at the tips, and never back to bare wood, or you'll lose it completely; deciduous hedges need to be cut back to 1 ft/30 cm the first year to encourage lateral growth. Just pinch off untidy shoots in following years to keep bushy. After that trim normally in June or early July.

* Keep the image of an A in mind as you clip, so the lower branches get some light.

HERBS

Herbs make wonderful ornamental plants. Most are scented and can be eaten, used as medicine or dried. Most develop the best flavor when they have lots of light and heat. Place stones between plants to build up warmth. One part of my garden is set out in a checkerboard pattern of paving stones. I plant my herbs in the spaces in between. The heat of the day is conserved well into the night. I whack away at them all summer, although I'm careful with the woody ones. The more you prune, the more you get. Non-woody herbs such as mint, chives and lemon balm can be cut back constantly.

* Herbs make beautiful arrangements, and you can dry any herb in your garden. You can tell if it's a herb by crushing a leaf—it will have a scent. Each plant has its own time for harvest, so you have to watch them.

* Seed herbs, such as dill, should be picked early in the morning, after they've lost their greenness but before they drop of their own accord. Spread them out to dry in the sun and store in bottles away from light.

* To improve flavor, treat herbs with an occasional dose of Epsom Salts. Mix 2 tbsp/25 mL Epsom Salts in 1 gal/4 L water and give them a deep drink. This will produce sturdier stems, stronger growth and make

them much more resistant to marauding insects. Better scent as well.

* They are spiciest for drying just before the flowers open

* To dry the seeds of herbs, pick the whole plant and put it upside down in a paper bag. Make holes at the top to allow for air circulation and hang it up. As flower heads dry, the seeds will fall into the bag. Store seeds in airtight jars in a cool, dry place.

* Herbs need four hours of sunlight a day and will thrive even in poor soil. (See individual herbs for special tips on care.)

* For eating, cut them back before blooms form.

* Herbs for shady places: mints, sweet cicely, sweet woodruff, angelica, comfrey, ginger and wintergreen.

* Use *Marrubium vulgare*, horehound, as a repellent against grasshoppers.

* If you want to bring herbs indoors for the winter, make sure you can provide the four hours of sunlight a day they require. Otherwise you have to use lights. The following are successful indoor pot plants for the winter:

* Rosemary—has to be brought indoors: it's a Mediterranean plant and can take some cold. Keep humid, and don't overwater.

* Thyme, sage, parsley, chives, tarragon—cut back one-third before bringing them indoors. Start them in pots several weeks before you start hardening them off for the trip inside.

* Rule of thumb—water plants with light delicate leaves more often than those with thick leaves. If there's a prolonged period of cloudy weather, cut back on watering all plants. Pruned plants need less water than those with lots of top growth.

* To test for watering, stick your finger in the soil to the first knuckle. If it's dry, water just until it comes out the drainage hole.

HORSERADISH *Armoracia rusticana*

Plant horseradish near your potatoes to protect them against blister beetle.

* Slugs are attracted to horseradish. Use it to draw them out so they'll be easy to bump off.

HORSETAIL *Equisetum*

Pick several dry leaves and boil in 1 cup/250 mL water for 20 minutes. The silica content makes this a good spray to combat powdery fungus on most plants and curly leaf on peach trees.

* Use to control mildew on roses and vegetables.

HOSTAS

Hostas are the ideal shade plant. They are ornamental, the flowers (and leaves) are lovely in bouquets and they can make some perfectly sane people go a bit addled. They range in size from small edgers to giant specimen plants in colors that are a dazzling array of yellows, blues, greens and variegations.

* To keep them looking neat, you've got to hit the slug patrol. Slugs are about the only enemy these plants have. Be prepared to handpick. They won't die from slugs, but they sure do look sickly. See also SLUGS.

* To keep the foliage from being splashed with mud during rainy weather, spread a thick layer of mulch underneath the leaves.

* The combination of hostas and ferns is one of the most enchanting parts of my woodland garden. The contrast between dense and light foliage, light-colored hostas and deep green ferns is touchingly beautiful. Hostas also work as a lower storey for tall plants such as *Thalictrum*, meadow rue; *Rodgersia*; *Polygonatum*, Solomon's seal.

* Hostas are great container plants. They put up with the worst kind of abuse and still look good. To winter them over, let them go dormant. Store in a cool place with the container on bricks to keep from freezing, or tip them on their sides. Leave them alone until they break dormancy in spring.

* Let the size of the hosta dictate the size of the pot. Use soil-less soil and keep out of harsh sunlight. Slugs won't bother these hostas.

HOUSEPLANTS

I find it tough to cope with houseplants in addition to a complicated garden. However, I bring pots of herbs such as marjoram and bay laurel, along with whatever else is growing with them, in for the winter. I give them a good shower to get rid of any bugs that might want to come inside.

* Give them an occasional feed of mild seaweed fertilizer (about half the suggested mix)—but not if they

are in dormancy. A misty shower once a month helps them combat our dry houses and also keeps them looking fresh.

* Protect plants from bugs and pets by putting anything spicy hot, such as cayenne pepper, dry mustard or curry powder, on accessible surfaces.

Hyssop   *Hyssopus officialis*

This handsome plant with bright blue flowers attracts bees, which is a Good Thing in any garden. As a companion plant it is supposed to repel flea beetles and cabbage moth. I wouldn't care if it did nothing except grow and look good. A superb companion with just about anything, it will also lure butterflies and hummingbirds into the garden. It needs no special care except deadheading. A self-seeder, it doesn't take to being moved about and demands about two years before it blooms again.

Insecticidal Soap

Go cheap here. Use ordinary all-soap dishwashing liquid—Ivory is very good—but no detergents. Add 1 tbsp/15 mL to 1 gal/4 L water and spray everything. It won't hurt a thing and the effort will make you feel awfully useful. You clean up the garden in more than one way because this stuff upsets the insides of the local pest population. It also cleans off pollutants from the surfaces of plants.

Insecticide

Making your own insecticide will save you lots of money, and you will be completely sure you aren't cluttering up the environment with harmful chemicals.

* Cooking water from asparagus kills nematodes (bad ones) and protects the roots and leaves of tomatoes.
* To help control disease and insect pests try the following antifungal garlic/onion spray:

> 2 handfuls chopped green onion OR
> 4 cloves garlic, bruised
> Boiling water (to cover)

Pour boiling water over green onion or garlic. Cover, allow to steep for at least a day. Add ½ cup/125 mL of the infusion to 5 gal/20 L of fertilizer for a good fertilizer tea. See also INTEGRATED PEST MANAGEMENT; PEST MANAGEMENT.

INSECTS, BENEFICIAL

Beneficial insects include ladybugs, parasitic wasps and lacewing fly.

* Beneficial insects can be attracted to the garden with the following spray:

> 2 tbsp/25 mL brewer's yeast
> ¼ cup/50 mL sugar
> 1 tsp/5 mL honey
> ⅓ cup/75 mL warm water

Mix together all ingredients. Dilute 1 tbsp/15 mL to 2 cups/500 mL water; spray on plants in spring and early summer to attract beneficial bugs.

* This same brew set into the ground attracts slugs, which will gobble it up and die in ecstasy.

INTEGRATED PEST MANAGEMENT

IPM is a term you'll be hearing more of in the future. It's a new "old" notion—in horticulture everything old seems new again. It's cheaper and ultimately more effective to work with nature than against it.

The wisdom of the ages now also has strong scientific backing.

* A lot of gardening is about attitude, and if you are fairly relaxed about the damage some pests do, your vegetables will produce higher yields. Moderate insect damage causes the plants to throw more energy into their defense system and produce larger seeds for survival.

* IPM works toward a balanced ecosystem in your garden. Wiping out all predators will also wipe out all beneficials at the same time. IPM is a combination of biological, physical and natural chemical insect and disease control. Control is the operational word, not eradication. Aphids attract ladybugs, for instance. Earwigs eat aphids and other pests. Getting rid of all your earwigs or aphids would not be doing your garden a big favor. (So far, however, slugs mystify me. Birds like them.)

* Encourage predators to come into the garden and prey on pests instead of knocking off the latter with noxious chemicals. These bugs are called beneficials.

* Some pests can be lured away from one plant to another. Beneficial plants include yellow marigolds, daisies, butterfly weed, tansy, fennel, cosmos, red zinnia, dwarf morning glories. Nasturtiums attract aphids. Mustard attracts many sucking insects.

* Beneficial bugs: Ladybugs, or lady beetles, are at the top of the list of all beneficial insects. But there is a long list to be considered: Ichneumonid wasp parasitizes 27 species of moths and butterflies that are destructive to plants. It lays eggs in tobacco budworms. See also INSECTS, BENEFICIAL; PEST MANAGEMENT.

* To achieve this balanced ecosystem, here's the ten-step method of an excellent book called *The 60-Minute Flower Garden* by Jeff Ball:

1. Maintain garden hygiene.
2. Rotate crops.
3. Build soil health.
4. Use interplanting and companion planting.
5. Learn pest emergence times and habits.

6. Use pest- and disease-resistant varieties.
7. Use biological controls.
8. Use physical controls.
9. Use natural sprays.
10. Use botanical poisons.

* Good soil will maintain active microlife in the top 6 in/15 cm, which includes all kind of predators.
* Pest emergence times:

asparagus beetle	late April through June
bean aphid	May and June
cabbage looper	May through July
corn earworm	July and August
Japanese beetle	June and July
Mexican bean beetle	May and June
spotted cucumber beetle	May and June
squash bug	May and June
squash vine borer	June and July
striped cucumber beetle	May and June

striped flea beetle	April and May
tomato hornworm	June through August

* Most gardens have only a few pests that are any danger. Know the pests of your area.
* Look up individual pests in this book for biological predators and controls that really do work. The more beneficials you have in the garden, the less likely you'll be overwhelmed with pests. Of course, once the pests are reduced, beneficials will wander off looking for them elsewhere.

See also COMPOST; MULCH; SOIL—the three major elements of the ecological garden.

INTERPLANTING OR INTERCROPPING

Nature fills any empty spaces around plants; something will move in to cover up the soil, and that something is usually weeds. By interplanting, even in the tiniest of vegetable gardens, no space needs to be wasted. The most beautiful gardens I've seen combine herbs, flowers and vegetables all in the same border. In these borders you can put plants together that are both beneficial and aesthetic.

* Combine plants that grow fast with those that are slower to sprout:
* Radishes and lettuce; green onions and beets.
* Plant spinach between rows of tomatoes.
* Grow green beans between rows of parsnips.
* Interplanting herbs and flowers improves garden health. Brassicas love the strongly scented herbs.
* Tomatoes protect roses from black spot.
* Corn will keep squash from wilting.
* Early spinach combines well with strawberries.
* Plant lettuce with peppers or among broccoli and cabbages.
* Put plants that need light in front of those that like to have some shade: Louise Riotte's best combinations are: asparagus with tomatoes, beans with carrots or summer savory, beets with onion or kohlrabi,

brassicas with aromatic plants or potatoes, leeks with onions, celery or carrots, turnips with peas.

* DON'T plant beans with onion, garlic or gladiolas; beets with pole beans; the brassicas with strawberries, tomatoes or pole beans; or potatoes with pumpkin squash, cucumber, sunflower, tomato or raspberry. These plants will inhibit each other's growth.

INVASIVE PLANTS

If your garden has to look after itself most of the summer, look to invasive plants. They will fill any space available, will survive on rainfall and generally don't need looking after: *Lysimachia clethroides*; *Oenothera*, evening primrose, are two to begin with. *Artemisia pontica* has feathery silver foliage. Many of the other artemisias such as *A. ludoviciana* 'Silver King' and 'Silver Queen' are gorgeous when mixed with other invasive plants such as mallow; *Macleaya*, plume poppy. *Fragaria*, both the ornamental and dessert strawberries, makes a swift ground cover. *Pulmonaria saccharata*, lungwort, with silver-dappled foliage will spread everywhere if you don't watch it. *Arabis caucasica*, rock cress, makes a sea of brilliant white flowers in spring that brings in the first crop of bees, adding sound to sight.

* If you want to grow beautiful but overly invasive plants such as mint or the variegated goutweed, *Aegopodium podagraria* 'Variegatum', plant them in pots with chicken wire plus 2 in/5 cm of gravel covering the bottom. Plunge the pot anywhere in the garden.

* *Sorbaria sorbifolia*, false spirea, is a ferny foliage with ecru silk plumes, and it spreads like crazy, making it a superb plant for the edge of the garden.

* Here's a list of invasives to avoid: Japanese knotweed, *Polygonum cuspidatum*; creeping bell flower, *Campanula rapunculoides*; and variegated goutweed *Aegopodium podagraria* 'Variegatum', which is the worst. It will choke out everything around in even dense, dry shade. Don't pull it out—snip at ground level until it

is dead, or cover with newspapers and plastic over at least one winter.

Crown vetch, *Coronilla varia*; Scotch broom, *Cytisus scoparius*; Dames's rocket, *Hesperis matronalis*; silver dollar plant, *Lunaria annua* are all quite capable of taking over.

JAPANESE BEETLE

Japanese beetle can be
affected by the following:
* Geraniums with roses and
grapes—which should drive the beetle away.
* Larkspur kills them; plant soybeans to act as a trap crop.
* It's the grub that's most destructive and should be
kept out of the garden at all costs. That's why you
may want to move to the killers of last resort. To
attack them, see BACCILUS POPILLIAE.

JEWELWEED   *Impatiens biflora*

This is one of those plants that the hortlorists love. It
really does relieve the itching from poison ivy.

* Collect as much jewelweed as you can and boil it in a pot of water until reduced. Strain, create a poultice, apply to the rash.
* If you've found poison ivy, you can probably find jewelweed, since they often grow near each other.

JUNE BEETLE

Also called June bugs, these bugs fly about in trees and around streetlights on fine June and July evenings. Watch out because they are probably planting eggs all over the garden and you'll find white grubs in late July or August. Apply controls such as Milky Spore Disease powder in midsummer before you are faced with dead or dying grass. Raccoons, birds and skunks will also quickly find that you have delicious grubs growing under the lawn.

Kitchen Waste

We are being swamped by garbage, and recycling kitchen waste is simple and responsible. Compost all your food scraps, coffee grounds, tea leaves, egg shells—but not fat, protein, dairy, meat, bones or oil. If you don't have a composter, bury waste in holes dug in the garden. Various bacteria turn garbage into lovely black compost within a year.

* Pick up an old blender in a garage sale and use it to mush up your wastes. This way, they'll break down much more quickly.

Knotweed *Polygonum aviculare*

An acid lover that, if it grows unbidden in your garden, will give you an idea of the pH of your soil. I've seen gardens hedged with knotweed so thick and high that it was an effective barrier against animals (and children, for that matter). In a small garden this plant is just too invasive. Use it where you want a wild effect or to cover up a bunch of junk—nothing will deter this plant.

* To get rid of knotweed, cut back each stem to 12 in/30 cm and coat with castor oil. Make sure the oil doesn't touch the surrounding soil or other plants by spreading a cloth around.

LACEWINGS

These beneficial bugs can be attracted into the garden with judicious plantings of any member of the carrot family, *Umbelliferae*: Queen Anne's lace, angelica, coriander, fennel. These bugs are also sold by mail. You'll recognize them by their long opaque green wings, ½ to ¾ in/12 to 18 mm long. The three to four generations they produce a year feed voraciously on aphids, corn earworms, mites, scale insects, white-flies, eggs of caterpillars, mites and thrips. They do most of their hunting in the last lar-val phase before adulthood. One larva will eat up to 60 aphids an hour.

* Diet: 1 part sugar to 1 part brewer's yeast in water, set near plants to encourage them to stay put.

LADYBUGS

First of all, you want to attract as many of these wonderful bugs to your garden as possible. Buying them by the bag is not necessarily the way to go. I've released thousands, and if the wind is wrong or the temperature not quite right or there aren't enough pests in the garden, they vanish or far too many of them keel over and die. When you do release purchased ladybugs, be as gentle as possible. If you can find out where they came from, this might be useful. Introducing them into a totally different climate isn't going to help them flourish. Try to get ladybugs from your own region or one with a similar climate.

* Release them at the base of plants plagued by aphids. They have insatiable appetites for these insects and will hang about until the aphids are polished off. By

then they will be acclimatized to your garden and probably stay.

* Plants to attract ladybugs: Queen Anne's lace, lamb's ears; nasturtiums; alfalfa; angelica; euonymous; goldenrod; morning glory; yarrow.

LAMB'S QUARTERS *Chenopodium album*

This annual weed produces a huge amount of seed, so be sure to keep it topped. Its presence indicates soil with lots of humus. A good companion with corn, cucumber, pumpkin, marigolds, peonies and pansies to protect soil.

* The early leaves can be added to salads and soups.

LANDSCAPING

There are many benefits from landscaping your property. It will probably raise its value, but far more important is what plants can do for your quality of life. For instance, deciduous trees on the south or west of the house act like giant air-conditioning units in summer. In winter they let in the sun for warmth.

* The windy side of the house can benefit from a windbreak planting that will reduce wind velocity up to 80 percent and save heating expense in winter.

* Just don't be boring and plant three shrubs and a tree in the front. Think about the style of your house very carefully and use as many native plants as you can when you install new plantings. In this way if you are hit with some weird weather, you can be assured that these plantings will remain the bones of your garden design. Keep in mind that shrubs and trees will probably grow faster than you think. At one time in my city, it was fashionable to plant blue spruce. Now there are thousands of houses swamped by these giant trees and they look ridiculous. And, of course, no one wants to cut down a mature tree and start again. You are making choices for a lifetime, so be careful.

* Light anything pale, such as birches, by back flood-lighting. Light up for drama. Christmas fairy lights slung over a shrub or in a tree look quite magical. You don't need expensive or elaborate methods to make your garden beautiful all year round.

LAVENDER *Lavandula*

Lavender is one of my favorite plants. I like to have as many kinds as possible. The one that seems to be the hardiest is *Lavandula angustifolia* 'Munstead'. If you find one that you like, take a cutting from it in spring by chopping off a woody piece and dipping the cut end in rooting hormone, then into a potting mix.

* Cut back in spring. You can be fairly savage and go to about 1 in/2.5 cm from the ground and it will come back from the roots. These plants loathe wet feet, but they can put up with fairly poor soil if they have at least four hours of sun a day.

* This is a good mouse repellent. It does work to

fend off moths in closets, but you have to replace it regularly.

* It is a superb edging plant and softens unattractive railway ties on raised beds.

LEAF CURL

Peach leaf curl looks crinkly and puckered. This is another of those diseases where the spores overwinter on the bark. The usual treatment is to use a fixed copper or lime sulphur fungicide during the winter. Make sure that all infected leaves are removed from the site.

* Prevent leaf curl on your peach tree by hanging mothballs around the tree.

* If leaf curl hits your rhododendrons (the leaves get swollen and then curl), handpick all the galls (the white spore formations) and destroy them.

* If you notice tightly curled leaves on raspberries, remove them immediately and get rid of the infected canes.

Leaf Miner

The trouble with this pest is that by the time you see their tunnels in the leaves of your flowers, especially lilacs, aquilegia, and vegetables, the damage is done. Look for bundles of white eggs on the underside of leaves in very early spring. You must remove any mess from your garden in fall to keep them from over-wintering. To prevent the spring arrival of these pests, cover seedlings with row covers after making sure there are no eggs on the leaves. Remove the covers once the plants are established.

Leafhoppers

Leafhoppers feed on beets, beans, celery, corn, lettuce and potatoes; rose leafhopper eats leaves of apple trees, cherry trees, maple trees, oak trees and strawberry plants; potato leafhopper feeds on potatoes, celery, eggplant and peanuts. They come in a variety of colors and suck chlorophyll, leaving small white or yellow spots on leaves and causing them to yellow and wilt, thereby stunting the plant's growth. They appear from April to May, excreting a sticky substance that attracts flies, wasps and ants. Make sure you clean up damaged leaves in fall and get rid of them.

* Weeds they love for laying eggs: oxalis, dock, shepherd's purse, pigweed, burdock and ragweed.
* Use insecticidal soap; hit the bug. One bite will spread any virus they are carrying. Be sure to cover the top and bottom of the plant.
* **Sabadilla spray—Mix 8 to 12 tbsp/125 to 175 mL Sabadilla dust in 1 gal/4 L water to make the spray.
* Dust plants with diatomaceous earth as long as it is dry.
* Natural insecticides need lots of reapplication.

* Enemies: green lacewings and ladybugs, predatory wasps, big-eyed flies.

LEAVES

Leaves are nature's wonder of wonders and your biggest asset in an ecological garden. They turn chlorophyll into sugar and when they fall off they break down and create humus. If the composter won't accommodate them all, dig a big hole and pile them in. They'll break down eventually and give you wonderful leaf mold for mulching.

* Or store in plastic bags with a little soil added. During the winter you can add this mixture to your composter along with your food scraps.

* Let leaves lie where they fall in paths in a woodland garden and they'll slowly break down to a soft 4 in/ 10 cm layer. The following spring, fork these leaves into the soil. A layer of leaves between rows of plants will keep them free of flying mud and weeds.

* If you can afford a leaf shredder it's probably a good investment, but if not try the following: Fill a large plastic garbage container with leaves (the lid will keep them dry). When it's full shove a weed trimmer up and down inside the container, shredding leaves as you go. It should take about five minutes to reduce the leaves to approximately an eighth of their volume. Be warned, the noise is excruciating.

LEEKS

Leeks must be blanched to get the white part we like to eat. Place a cardboard paper towel roll around the plant and pile dirt up the outside.

LETTUCE

Lettuce doesn't germinate well in midsummer heat. For summer sowing put seeds in a plastic bag with moist vermiculite and let them germinate in the fridge; this should take about a week. Then plant in a shady spot 6 in/15 cm apart.

* Side dress lettuces with manure, blood meal or fish emulsion once a month.

* Lettuce loves the shade and makes a lovely edging plant even if you never eat it. Or plant with taller plants.

LILIES

There is no tip to help the following problem, but it's wise to be on guard. If you see a beautiful red beetle with black legs anywhere near your lilies, you've been invaded by *Lilioceris lilii*, the lily-leaf beetle. It will ravage your lilies' leaves, stressing the plant almost to death. Bacillus thuringiensis might help but it can also harm beneficials. Handpicking seems the only way to go. The coral-colored larvae cover themselves with a black slime, making them disgusting to birds.

Make sure that there's no vegetable debris around the plants for adults to overwinter in.

* Fertilize with compost tea or aged manure once leaves show.

LOVAGE

This plant really does improve the health of a garden. It has tenacious roots, so it is probably wise to put it where it can stay or keep it in a permanent container.

* It's delicious chopped up in scrambled eggs.

Manure

Are you confused about manure? Well, sheep and cow manure are cold manure and good for light soil; horse manure is dry and good for heavy, cold or clay soils. In spring, spread well composted manure around the garden; in autumn, it's okay to apply fresh manure—winter frosts will help it break down. Manure contains nitrogen and is a fertilizer as well as a crackerjack soil amender.

* Chicken manure is high in nitrogen.
* Never use dog, cat or human manure.
* Manure tea: fill an old pillowcase with manure. Hang it in a garbage can filled with water for a couple of days, strain and then apply around shrubs and trees.
* Dilute manure tea 50–50 for perennials and containers.
* Never use it as a foliar spray.

MARIGOLDS *Tagetes*

There has been so much press about marigolds that I'm not sure what to believe anymore. They're supposed to suppress bad nematodes in everything from roses to potatoes to strawberries. Generally, they are planted with crops susceptible to nematode damage. Perhaps people are wary because it takes about two years for the chemical that marigolds exude to kick in. They've never done a lot for my garden, but there are ecological gardeners who swear by them and wouldn't be without them, especially around tomato plants.

* *Calendula officinalis*, pot marigold, is supposed to discourage dogs from whizzing on precious evergreens. It's probably more useful to chop up the blooms and drop them into salads. Very tasty.

MICE

I know little field mice are out there looking for a place to nest once the weather gets cold.

* Crush mint leaves and place near entry spots to discourage mice from coming into the house. Wormwood and spurge repel field mice from the garden.

* Plant mint to keep mice and other rodents away from your compost pile.

* Deep mulching encourages mice to nest in the cozy warmth provided by you, the great steward of the garden. This is the main reason not to pile it up against low branches or the trunks of trees and shrubs.

* Mice won't bother with the following plants: daffodils, narcissus, scilla, grape hyacinth.

* Coat the rim of a pail with peanut butter and balance a ruler over the edge. When the mouse walks along it, the fulcrum changes and the mouse drops into the water. If you can, save the mouse and release outdoors.

* Gum candy, such as wine gums, stuck to a trap will hold a mouse in place.

* Voles are field mice that like grasses; deer mice will eat seeds.
* House mice will eat anything and they are as smart as rats.

MICROCLIMATE

Each region has a general climate, then each garden has a microclimate of its own. It's influenced by how much light it gets, the prevailing winds, how high buildings and trees are around the house, the direction the garden faces, and what is in the garden in the way of trees and shrubs. Different parts of the garden will have their own, even smaller, microclimates if they are more sheltered than others. It can shift from a north-facing fence (cool, late to thaw) to a south-facing (warmer and loses snow earlier). Shady areas under trellises and arbors will be cooler.
* When you are planting the bones of your garden, stick to hardy well-tested plants or native trees and

shrubs. You will have a head start if any unexpected weather hits that might wipe you out. When starting from scratch, place trees so they will protect the garden from the prevailing winds. You will have shelter and be able to push the limits of your planting. A pond can make the surrounding area cooler in the day-time and warmer at night.

* Trees and shrubs can alter the garden radically. Huge trees will bring masses of moisture from deep in the ground and transpire so that the garden becomes much cooler. The shade will provide areas with slightly lower temperatures.

* Change your microclimate by adding a hedge. See HEDGES.

* Vines and tall plants add a bit of shade and absorb heat. Don't put tender vines on the side of your garden where winter winds come sweeping in. Use hardy vines that can withstand the onslaught.

* Paint fences a light color to reflect light and make the area below warmer.

* Dark colors absorb heat and radiate it in the

evening. Keep this in mind when you plant near them. Water requirements might go up.

* The density of a fence makes a difference. An open lattice fence lets in both light and wind, providing less protection than a high, dense wooden fence. I have a square open trellis fence on the north side of my lot even though this is where the winds come from. It's for aesthetic purposes rather than protection. But we are at the bottom of a ridge and there are mature trees all about, so I'm not worried about severe frost damage.

* Fences on the south side of property will be the first to freeze in fall and the last to thaw in spring. Take this into account when you plant bulbs.

* Keep a record and track when the first and last frosts come into your garden. The most efficient way is to get one of those thermometers that record the high and low temperature each day. I find that by recording the daily temperatures, the hours of sunlight, depth of rain and the humidity, I have a really good idea of what I can and cannot do at any time. I also

keep a record of what's in bloom, how plants perform and when I move them about. My garden is fluid in the extreme.

MILDEW

Spores of this fungi are carried by the wind, settling on leaves and sending out mycelia (little white threads) that cover the leaves with a white coat. Then it sends suckers into the plant's sap, and the overwintering black spores take over. Mildew is a secondary problem in many cases. It grows on leaves coated by the secretion of aphids or scale. Get rid of the latter and you will safeguard against the former.

* Mildew can be headed off with a spray of 1 tbsp/ 15 mL baking soda in a quart/liter of water. It can be safely used on most plants.

* A tea made with horsetail is also a good spray. Cover the horsetail with water and let ferment for 10 days. Dilute in the same ratio as above.

* Mustard seed flour mixed with water is also useful as a spray.
* Sulphur dust is very effective.
* Quite often plants such as phlox that suffer from mildew will improve if you move them to a spot where they have better air circulation. In spring, lots of water when they need it along with a compost mulch will help the plant maintain its health and ward off this fungus.

MILKY SPORE DISEASE.
See BACILLUS POPILLIAE

MINERALS

Many plants contain minerals that make them invaluable for the compost. Any plant such as dandelion that has a tap root long enough to reach down into the hardpan where minerals reside will bring minerals up to the surface. This may also explain why vegetables grown near weeds often are the tastiest.

* Rocks add minerals to the soil. Finely ground phosphate rock consists largely of calcium phosphate with some trace minerals that will be available to the plant as needed. Ten lb/5 kg per 100 sq ft/9 sq m is recommended by Rodale.

* Superphosphate has been treated with sulphuric acid to make it more soluble. It becomes both a water-soluble phosphate and calcium sulphate, highly soluble, but lacks the trace minerals necessary for healthy plants.

* Potash contributes a wide variety of minerals and is one of the three major nutrients essential for plant growth and disease resistance. It's found in manure, compost and plant residues. Granite dust will provide it if there's a deficiency in the soil.

* Lime is used mainly to raise the pH to make the soil more alkaline. Ground limestone is the best form and it helps release some of the phosphorus and potash in

the soil. Add to freshly cultivated soil. Wood ash, ground oyster shells and crystallized marble are all forms of limestone.

* Dolomite contributes calcium, magnesium, potassium and trace elements needed by plants.

MINT

Mint is extremely invasive but it is one of the few herbs that does well in shade. If you have a very small garden, grow mint in pots and plunge them into the ground. Take vegetative cuttings in fall to grow for next year.

* There are at least a dozen kinds of mint now available in nurseries, from apple to pineapple to variegated.

* Mints, like tomatoes, have an affinity for stinging nettle.

* To keep mint under control, cut all around the clump with a shovel in the spring. During the season, whack back at least once a month.

* Use mint to get rid of white cabbage worm; it repels the butterflies.
* Peppermint needs lots of humus and water. But it keeps red ants away from shrubs and white cabbage butterflies from cabbages.
* Spearmint keeps aphids off nearby plants; ants hate mint and thereby keep their aphids off mint plants.
* Plant mint to keep mice and other rodents away from your compost pile.
* Mint is considered by some herbal mavens as the best of all plants to hold back hills from erosion. This does describe how hardy it is and how much mint will spread if it's allowed.
* I plant mine in spaces left open between patio stones and have a collection of mints and basils in pots. Stick to one mint per pot so you don't get confused by the subtle differences.

MIRRORS

Mirrors shouldn't be confined to the indoors. Placed properly, they are a splendid way of making a deck or even a small garden look wider or deeper. I now have mirrors placed throughout the garden to create the illusion of space. One slants slightly so that I can see all the bright red twigs of a dogwood and the dense maroon of mahonia. It also makes the garden look fuller in winter.

* Mirrors can be used to double the effect of light on seedlings. Position the mirror so light from the sun or a fluorescent lamp will be reflected back onto the seedlings.

MITICIDE

To deal with spider mites, make the following spray:

    2 tbsp/25 mL flour
        1 qt/1 L water
    1 tbsp/15 mL milk

Mix flour, water and milk. Spray on the underside of plants at the first sign of infestation.

Mixed Borders

An all-annual or perennial border is very traditional in North America, but I like gardens that are a blend of everything. It not only makes for a much longer season but can, in fact, be more easily planned for year-round interest.

* Mix a few evergreen shrubs into your flower bed for winter appeal.

* Add large rocks or stepping stones with unusual shapes and textures.

* Heathers are nice for medium to small beds. These tend to look best in threes, unequally spaced or in a clump. In larger beds go to the next odd number (five, seven and so on). Make sure the soil is acidic.

* I picked up this tip from a wise gardener with a wonderful garden. She hates spending a lot of money

on plants. When she wants to put in shrubs, instead of getting a large expensive one, she buys three small ones. She gets the immediate effect she wants, and when they get crowded, she removes the middle one and places it somewhere else in the garden. This is a great idea if you have lots of space.

Moles

I know that moles can be destructive, though I have no experience with them so far (just raccoons, skunks and squirrels). Place 2 to 3 tbsp/25 to mL diatomaceous earth in each tunnel and push the soil down until the tunnels are blocked. They tend not to reuse these tunnels. By systematically blocking the tunnels, maybe you'll discourage them.

* *Euphorbia lathyris,* caper spurge or mole plant, is supposed to deter moles and if placed with narcissus and castor bean plants makes an effective barrier around the garden against these pests.

* Stick thorny twigs from raspberry canes and roses into the mouths of holes and hope that these rascals will give themselves a good scraping.

* Set a pop bottle in the soil with the mouth just above the ground. When the wind blows the bottles will whistle and irritate the animal. Of course, it may drive you nuts. And if you adjust, the mole might too.

* Once again, garlic to the rescue: crush several whole heads of garlic and stick the mash into mole tunnels. They don't like the smell.

* All the other solutions I've heard about are so destructive and violent I hate to mention them.

MONARDA DIDYMA　Bee balm, Oswego tea

This plant really does attract bees to the garden,

which, in turn, speeds up pollination of the other plants around it. Plant *Monarda* near tomatoes and it will improve their flavor.

MONOGARDENING

Monogardening is one of those trends that looked like it was going to take off a few years ago. Choose a color and use that as your theme. It was made popular by Vita Sackville-West when she worked out her famous white garden at Sissinghurst. Using only one color really highlights the wide range of tones in a single color. My own preference is to have lots of blue in the garden closest to the deck. In fact, at some seasons of the year this area is almost all blues, silvers and grays, which is about as close to monogardening as I like to get.

* If you decide to have a monogarden, start with one border and see how you like the effect. You still have to think of every season and what will come up, when, and how intense it will be. Combining within

the same color means you have to be really careful. For instance, if you decide to have an all-red border, watch how you put reds with a lot of blue in them with those that have a lot of yellow.

* Create a pink garden, a white one, or mostly blue (hard because blue is the most difficult color to find) or even a yellow garden.

* Think carefully about the foliage in a monogarden or border. Use gray foliage plants as background, to lower the intensity of a hue or create a pattern or thread through the area to give the eye a rest.

Moon Signs

Gazing at the moon should be part of your gardening practice. The moon has gravitational pulls on the earth, so during a full moon, soil moisture rises closer to the earth's surface. Since seeds need moisture to break dormancy, it makes sense for speedy germination to sow them with the full moon.

* How to predict summer weather? If the horns or tips of the new moon point upward, it will be a dry summer; if they point down, it will be a wet summer.
* Harvest during the dark of the moon (last quarter to emerging new moon).
* Start compost when the moon is in the fourth quarter.
* Fertilize when the moon is in Cancer, Scorpio or Pisces—all fruitful signs.
* Rudolph Steiner developed biodynamic gardening, which follows the alignment of moon and planets for planting and harvesting. Look for his books, which are really fascinating if you want to explore this concept.

MORNING GLORIES *Ipomoea purpurea*

In the city I live in you will see many fanciful uses for morning glories. I've seen pergolas covered with them; awnings created by vine-covered lines coming

away from the house; fences smothered in them.
Grow vegetables with them as well.

* They are so easy to grow from seed. Pour boiling
water over the seed to speed up germination. Then
plant. This is a potential reseeder but next year's crop
is less likely to be as good.

* These flowers are ideal for children to grow in their
own gardens, since the action is pretty swift and the
results flashy.

MOSQUITOES

Remember the days when ponds everywhere were rit-
ually covered with kerosene and oil to keep mosquito
larvae from developing? If you have a pond on your
property and are worried about mosquitoes breeding, pour a garlic-based oil over the surface during
the breeding season. It's less destructive and just as
effective.

Adding fish, of course, is the best way to go. Make sure the pond is 2 to 3 feet deep.

* Take West Nile Virus seriously; never go outside without applying insect repellent; wear long-sleeved clothes.

Moss

Moss makes almost any area look established. If cracks develop in the surface of your walk or drive-way, in spring, pour buttermilk in the lesions and sprinkle a bit of live moss on them; the moss will grow and give the area an aged patina.

* This method of growing moss also works on stones and stone furniture: mix live moss and buttermilk, add a little yogurt and glop onto the surface. Be patient. Continue the treatment after every rainfall until the moss is growing. Be persistent.

* There are two types of mosses: tuft-forming have

rhizoids running along the surface of the shoot; bud-forming make a carpet of moss.

* If you receive moss or find some growing on your property and want to expand it, try the following: Choose a weed-free spot well protected from the wind; never under the dense shade of conifers. They can survive under maples, unlike a lot of other plants. Take a small piece and keep it moist. Because moss has no specialized cells, each cell is capable of growing a new plant, so you don't need a large piece. Soak the soil, press the moss in place. Water until the edges have established themselves.

* Repair damaged moss by adding a solution of 1 part buttermilk and 7 parts water, for a few weeks in spring. This will help acidify soil. Keep weeds out by lopping off the tops until the weeds die.

* All of this is wonderfully romantic, of course, because if you have raccoons or squirrels sharing your garden the sight of moss makes them doubly curious. They'll take to lifting it up and tossing it around. The only way to combat this is to anchor it

in place with plastic mesh held down with bricks or heavy stones. Once established it should be okay.

MULBERRIES

I have an old weeping mulberry that the kids used to use as a fort. Now that they've left home, I've gotten rid of it. Its great virtue was that the berries attracted birds. Squirrels had a go at them as well. A mulberry keeps the wildlife happy so they might not touch your other plants. They will, however, seed all over the place and you must keep them properly pruned and get rid of the seedlings. Service-berry is a much better plant. See page 284.

MULCH

Mulch is any organic matter piled up around your plants that slowly breaks down and provides food for the soil. It is magic for the garden and in my mind an absolutely integral part of all good gardening practice.

* When you mulch, think of the forest with its layers of litter from fallen leaves and needles. If I had this throughout my garden, I'd be very happy. But three-quarters-finished compost is a superb substitute. Next, cocoa bean hulls, even though the aroma puts you off eating chocolate for at least a week, mixed with sheep manure; finely ground wood chips, not the big chunks; pine needles along with evergreen boughs; a combination of grass clippings and chopped-up weeds. If available, salt hay, seaweed and straw are excellent.

*My favorite mulch is one third each of cocoa fiber, ground-up leaves and compost.

* Mulch keeps the ground cool, discourages weeds,

cuts down on watering and is a fine background for plants. Here are some general rules:

* Mulch after the ground has frozen in fall, and after plants have shown new growth in spring. For the best effect use a minimum depth of 2 in/5 cm and up to 4 in/10 cm of mulch.

* Organic mulch on your beds eliminates the need for deep tilling and cultivating. Therefore you won't disturb delicate root systems. In breaking down, an organic mulch will constantly feed the soil and provide it with nutrients as they are needed. This is not a fast hit, and you shouldn't look for instant results.

* Keep mulch at least a good inch/2.5 cm away from rosettes or any obvious cluster of leaves or tops of plants, and from stems and trunks. This prevents any possibility of rot setting in and deters pests that like to spend their winters in this cozy environment.

* Place a mulch of comfrey around potatoes to provide potassium and to hold moisture in the soil.

* Protect vegetables from overnight frosts in fall with a blanket of loose hay; remove in the morning. We

used to pile hay up over carrots and they were good for harvesting most of the winter.

* Be careful when using the very large bark chips that can be purchased by the bag. They can dry out the soil something fierce, and I don't think they look particularly attractive. Finely shredded bark is more permeable and better looking.

* Plant perennials such as Ladino clover for a living mulch. Leave it the following season as a green manure; turn under the following year. This is for large properties.

* Plant straight into the clover—dig holes or till strips and go right ahead and plant into the year-old crop.

* Clover mulch makes a superb bed for corn, which is a heavy user of nitrogen.

* Mulch for blueberries—the best is sawdust, and it's beginning to look promising for strawberries and other small crop fruit as well.

* Coir, coconut fiber, is a renewable resource, which will hold water and cut down on watering.

MUSTARD

Mustard can be planted as a trap crop to draw insects away from vegetables. It's considered a host plant for insects and must be removed and destroyed as soon as it becomes infested.

NARCISSUS

These glorious plants are *supposed* to be poisonous to squirrels. I say supposed because I've had years of squirrel overpopulation and these little creatures will dig them up and throw them around. However, if you plant a few narcissus with your tulips, the squirrels will not necessarily ravage the tulips.

* Names: 'Minnow', 'Jack Snipe', 'Thalia' and 'Cheerfulness'.

* Plant *Tagetes erecta*, African marigold, or *T. patula*, French marigold, in the bed with the narcissus to kill off nematodes that might attack the bulbs.

Nasturtiums

These are wonderful annuals, especially the pretty pink-red and subtle cream forms. Any nasturtium attracts aphids to its flowers and, therefore, it's known as a trap plant. The aphids attract ladybugs, and once they've bumped off the aphids on this plant they look around for aphids on all the other plants.

* Nasturtiums discourage whitefly in greenhouses.
* Plant near squash to keep squash bugs away.
* Nasturtiums indicate that the soil has a lime deficiency.
* Make a spray with nasturtium leaves (chop, boil and strain, with a bit of soap so it will stick). Spray vegetables and flowers to improve growth and flavor.
* Plant near broccoli, potatoes, radishes, brassicas and under trees to ward off woolly aphids.
* Plant in poor soil for lots of bloom.
* Deadheading is essential. Grow in either sun or part shade.

Naturalized Plantings

One of the most incredible sights in spring is a field or
garden with naturalized plantings that look as though
the wind had swept them into place. All too often
bulbs, such as daffodils, planted in lawns and mead-
ows look too studied. I usually put them in a basket,
toss them out to roll in whatever direction they fancy
and plant where they lie. Or toss pebbles or marbles
over your shoulder; plant a bulb where each drops.

* Place native plants in an area to be naturalized.
They have had millennia to develop genes that allow
them to survive.

* Some plants are thought to be native because
they've been in an area for such a long time—but
they might have come over on shipments of eigh-
teenth-century grain, in the pockets of a nineteenth-
century farmer or only during this century. Join a
native plant society and learn about which ones are
truly native to your area.

* Rip out the grass and go native. There will be wild-

flower beauty, some plants that others think are weeds (don't listen) and shrubs and trees that can withstand local conditions. This will vary from coast to coast; there are no hard and fast rules, but here's what I do:

* Look at the natural plantings in fields and forests in your region. From these observations make a sensible list of plants including trees and shrubs. Check out how they are combined in nature and try to emulate this as much as possible.

* If you have a garden full of what you think are weeds, chances are you have lots of native plants. Isolate the most interesting patches by cutting around them and identify the plants. If they are native species you want, leave them in place or divide and move to your native garden. I'd start with *Rudbeckia hirta*, Black-eyed Susan—it attracts good bugs, looks beautiful and combines well with just about anything.

* Most municipalities are changing their laws so that it is now legal to have a naturalized or native garden—but check first.

* Avoid meadow-in-a-can. You don't know what's in there and it will be nothing but Queen Anne's lace in three years.

NEMATODES

These small almost thread-like worms are everywhere—in soil, water, animals and plants. Alex Shigo, one of the masters of tree biology, writes, "Some forms have mouth parts that look like an open tube. They suck in fungus spores, and other small bits of organic matter like a miniature vacuum cleaner. . . . The other type has mouth parts that look like a needle. . . . These forms stick the needle into plant parts and suck materials."

* Bad nematodes attack fine tree roots, transmit diseases and can wound plants. Keep them under control by planting marigolds, salvia, dahlias and asparagus. These are natural nematicides (which explains why tomatoes grown near these plants are

protected from asparagus beetle). Add lots of humus and compost to help soil keep bad nematodes in check.

* Good nematodes are a boon to gardeners. These parasitic nematodes are turning into safe biological control agents. They attack only insects and aren't harmful to humans, pets, earthworms, birds, honeybees or beneficial insects above the soil surface. They strike the disgusting grubs that turn into Japanese beetle and are useful in controlling borers, root weevils, cutworms, beetle grubs, gnats, cabbage root maggots, black vine weevils and wireworms.

* Nematodes should be applied when soil temperature is above 55°F/12°C. Soil should be moist, almost wet.

* Here is a fact you may never use: Any insect that goes through its entire life cycle above the ground will not come in contact with soil-dwelling nematodes.

Some nematode products: Biosafe; Scanmask.

NESTS FOR BIRDS

Supplying building material helps attract birds to the garden. Save all loose threads and snippets of yarn and roll into loose balls. In spring, hook these wads onto twigs in trees. Birds, no fools, prefer natural fibers such as cotton and wool.

NETTLE

This useful plant stimulates the growth of any other plants around it.

* Throw chopped-up nettles into the composter to hurry the decomposition process.
* Currant bushes are said to fruit better and be more resistant to disease if there are nettles nearby.
* Though they may be painful, they do provide a home for butterfly pupae.

NITROGEN

Nitrogen is one of the main elements of life. Without it neither we nor the plants we grow would survive. It is essential for plant growth. A nitrogen-deprived plant will turn yellow. If there's too much nitrogen, the green matter becomes mushy and floppy and goes yellow, especially on the old leaves nearest the bottom of the plant. Eighty percent of the atmosphere is nitrogen, which plants can't get at until there's been a thunder and lightning storm, or it's washed out of the atmosphere in the form of rain or snow.

* Good sources of nitrogen are blood meal and, to a lesser extent, manure such as chicken, horse, sheep and cow in descending order. Use as a side dressing on vegetables once a month in good soils or twice a month in poor soil throughout the growing season because vegetables are heavy nitrogen users.

* There are plants with nodules of nitrogen in their roots: beans, clover, peas, peanuts. These plants will benefit, as well as nearby plants.

* *Ilex verticillata*, winterberry, adds nitrogen to the soil.
* Trees that have pods are able to take nitrogen out of the air and store it in roots and stems. The pods fall, decay, and return nitrogen to the soil. The following trees have pods: *Robinia*; *Gleditsia*, honeylocust; *Gymnocladus dioica*, Kentucky coffee-tree; *Cercis canadensis*, redbud; *Cladrastis lutea*, yellowwood; *Genista tinctoria*, woadwaxen; *Amorpha fruticosa*, false indigo bush.

Northern Gardening

There is a strange fear of gardening in the very coldest parts of the country, yet here can be found some of the most interesting and adventurous gardening. The rigors of the climate seem to bring out the audacious side of any gardener.

* For really successful gardening in these areas, there are a few things to remember. One, observe the native

plants around you and see how they react to your climate. This is called phenology (see page 236). The other is that though there are fewer growing days, the longer days make it possible to grow most hardy annuals, vegetables, perennials and foliage plants.

* Knowing your microclimate, especially the first and last frost dates, is even more important in the north than in more temperate zones. Frost dates can be obtained by calling local agricultural stations, who have information on regional conditions. But even *more* important is to keep a record of daily temperatures in your own garden over a number of years. You'll be surprised how consistent weather really is. The temperatures in your own garden can vary quite widely from that of gardens

down the street simply because, say, you have a few trees better placed to ward off the prevailing winds. See also MICROCLIMATE; HEDGES; WINDBREAKS.

* Many bulbs and lilies can be planted right up until hard frost. Prepare the holes ahead of time and check that the drainage is good (just pour water into the hole to be sure it goes away in a matter of minutes). Add a little bone meal to the bottom of the hole, though this isn't really that important the first year. Store the saved soil where it won't freeze. It's easy enough, once you receive the bulbs, to pop them into place, fill with soil, press down and leave them alone.

* The same principle can be used for shrubs and trees once they've gone into dormancy. But don't plant evergreens after even a light frost. They don't go into dormancy and the roots will not only go into shock, they may freeze up.

* Remember that the wind is your number-one enemy—even more than fiercely low temperatures. Plant windbreaks first and then get on with the rest of your garden.

This is where adjusting your microclimate is incredibly important. Make sure that you haven't placed your garden right in a frost hollow—heavy cold air is likely to sink like a stone onto lower ground. Fences, hedges and small buildings act as shelters and create warmer spaces around themselves. And be prepared to wrap your plants for a couple of years until they get totally adjusted to your garden. Revolting but necessary, alas. See BURLAP-WRAPPED PLANTS.

* Sun scald is the next most important thing, especially in March when the sun can practically fry a plant. Protect vulnerable plants by combining them with larger plants so they can be both shaded and protected from wind. Tie Christmas tree branches on the south side of plants to keep the spring sun at bay.

* Snow is the best mulch of all, and if you have more than 6 in/15 cm of snow on the ground all winter you are in good shape to hang on to all deciduous plants. Since they retreat underground at the first sign of frost, they are essentially protected. If you are subjected to periods of freezing followed by thaws—I'm thinking here of the Rockies and the famous Chinook winds—you will have to mulch very deeply. Don't go into winter without giving plants, especially evergreens, a good soak and a blanket of mulch at least 4 in/10 cm deep to keep the temperature of the soil even. As long as the temperature remains even, the living tissue will remain comfortable.

* If you grow your own seeds, warm up the water before you give your seedlings a drink. Even getting it to room temperature will prevent some shock.

* Always select plants that are designated as hardy. Don't worry if some plants get killed back each year. They will probably come back from the roots. Don't get discouraged and start pulling things out. I usually leave things in place for a couple of years in hope that something might stir in the root zone. Whenever I've deviated from this rule, I've regretted it. I had a *Corylus avellana* 'Contorta', corkscrew hazel, that I moved to three different locations trying to get it right. In its last resting place it looked quite dead, so I started to pull it out. To my astonishment there was growth on

the side that was hidden from view. All this yanking killed the plant, so I used the corpse as an ornament in a big pot for winter interest.

* The smaller and more ground hugging a plant, the more likely that it will survive prairie and Arctic winds.

* Plants for cold areas:

* Trees: *Juniperus scopulorum* 'Tolleson's Blue Weeping', Rocky Mountain juniper; *Larix decidua*, larch; *L. sibirica*, larch. (Larch is a deciduous conifer.) *Picea abies* 'Nidiformis', nest spruce; *P. glauca* 'Caerulea', white spruce; *P. g. albertiana* 'Conica', Dwarf Alberta spruce; *P. pungens* 'Glauca Iseli Fastigiata', Colorado blue spruce; *P. p.* 'Globosa', Colorado spruce; *Pinus mugo*, Mugho pine; *P. m.* 'Flat Top'; *P. strobus* 'Pendula', weeping white pine; *P. sylvestris* 'Nana', dwarf Scotch pine; *Microbiota decussata*, Siberian cedar.

* Ornamental grasses: *Helictotrichon*; *Bromus*; *Arrhenatherum*; *Deschampsia*; *Alopecurus*; *Briza*; *Phalaris arundinacea*.

* Vines: *Celastrus scandens*, American bittersweet;

Clematis such as 'Jackmanii', 'Ville de Lyon', 'Etoile Violette' are hardy; *Lonicera brownii* 'Dropmore Scarlet Trumpet'; *Parthenocissus quinquefolia*, Virginia creeper; *P. q.* 'Engelmannii' Engleman ivy.

* Shrubs: *Azalea* 'Apricot Surprise'; *Rhododendron carolinianum* 'PJM'; *Genista lydia*, dwarf broom; *Euonymus alata*, burning bush (fantastic fall color); *E. nana* 'Turkestanica'; *Shepherdia argentea* (This wonderful silver plant puts out suckers, so plant it as a wind break); *Caragana arborescens*, Siberian pea tree (Almost all members of this family work well in areas from zone 2); *Prunus tomentosa*, Nanking cherry; *P. besseyi*, Western sandcherry; *Cotoneaster acutifolius*, Peking cotoneaster (the black berries are gorgeous); *C. integerrimus*, European cotoneaster; *C. horizontalis*, rock cotoneaster; *Viburnum dentatum*, arrowwood; *V. trilobum*, highbush cranberry; *V. t.* 'Compactum' and 'Nanum'; *Ribes alpinum*, alpine currant; *R. aureum* (a very fragrant golden form); *R. missouriense*; *Daphne cneorum*; *Forsythia ovata* 'Northern Gold'; *Hydrangea paniculata*

'Grandiflora', Peegee hydrangea; *Salix purpurea* 'Nana', dwarf willow; *Symphoricarpos albus*, snowberry. Many other shrubs are ideal for cold temperatures: lilac, mock orange, potentilla, spirea, Russian olive, sea buckthorn, sumach and weigela.

* Many deciduous perennials need only a thick layer of mulch (4 in/10 cm) or snow to bring them through winter successfully. Weather will never discourage a crazed gardener.

* Always check where your plants come from. If you live in Saskatchewan or North Dakota and the plants come from Oregon or British Columbia, you might be in for trouble. Supporting your local nurseries is the wisest choice for cuttings. If you want to try something new and different, grow from seed. And save those bills. Usually they are your guarantee.

* Make sure that the bones of your garden consist of tested native hardy plants. You don't want this part of your garden wiped out because of unusual conditions.

Oak

Oak leaves make great acid mulch. They are slow to break down, so it's best to chop them up before spreading them around acid-loving plants. They perk up *Pieris japonica*, kalmias, rhodos and azaleas.

* Oak mulch controls the growth of maggots in turnips and radishes. And slugs are supposed to be repelled by it. In my experience nothing repels slugs, but try oak mulch for cutworms and June bug grubs.

* To keep oak trees healthy, encourage trichogramma wasps, whose larvae feed on gypsy moth eggs. Bacillus thuringiensis kill caterpillars in these trees.

* Oak trees have a large amount of calcium in the bark, ash from these trees is high in calcium. Use oak wood ash in the compost.

ONIONS

If you plant onions around the garden, you will confuse insect pests and they may leave other vegetables alone. Because of their shallow roots, it's possible to plant them almost anywhere.

* Planted near lettuce, onions have been found to keep slugs away.

* If you want large onions, start feeding them nitrogen fertilizers two weeks after transplanting.

* Onions and brassicas are wonderful companions.

* Onion maggots can travel, so set onions in with other plants such as tomatoes, lettuce and strawberries.

* When onions are cut, they exude propanethial S-oxide, which is the stuff that makes your eyes water. (Try peeling them under water.) But this makes them a good natural pesticide. A little onion juice mixed with some soap in water is an excellent spray.

* Don't cover up onions when you cultivate them. Remove the soil from the top and they'll grow nice and big.

* Alliums are in the onion family. Plant different species for each season. The small *A. moly* look great under roses and 'Purple Sensation' adds a masterly touch with shrubs and trees.

ORACH   *Atriplex hortensis*

This gorgeous annual herb not only is good in cooking but also marries well with many other herbs. It is beet red, has ruffled leaves and grows to about 7 ft/2 m. Combined with bronze fennel, blue salvia and *Allium sphaerocephalum*, it is striking in any border.

OREGANO   *Origanum vulgare*

I like the yellow version of this aromatic herb. It makes a smashing clump and fits in well with grasses, evergreens and certainly other herbs.

* Plant it with cabbages to repel cabbage butterfly.
* *Origanum vulgare* 'Aureum' is the bright yellow cultivar of the species and it makes a splendid slow-growing clump. Keep it chopped back for good form.

PARSLEY

What a great plant. This biennial is attractive in containers and makes a feathery contrast with the more formal foliage of basil. I like both the curly and Italian types.

* Parsley is notoriously difficult to germinate. Place the seeds on a sheet of sandpaper and rub them vigorously with another piece of sandpaper. Freeze the seeds for a week. Just before planting, pour boiling water over them.

* Mix parsley with carrot seed to repel carrot flies by masking the carrot aroma.

* Plant next to roses to guard against rose beetle.

* Plant with tomatoes or asparagus to make them stronger.

* Plants about to bolt can be cut for a flower arrangement or added to kitty litter as a freshener.

PATINA

It takes a garden about five to six years to look settled, but you can age it by keeping as many old trees and shrubs as possible. Prune them to look gnarled, almost like giant bonsai.

* Then move on to the artifacts you put into the garden. A patina looks wonderful on concrete furniture or steps, stoneware or clay pots. Get a weathered look by painting on a slurry (paste) of water and cow manure or live yogurt; or soot, manure and water. I have taken live mosses from between rocks, dried them, mixed them with buttermilk, then painted the mixture on for a good effect. See also AGING.

PEACH

Always use a lot of old composted manure around peach trees.

* Plant garlic near the trunks to inoculate the tree against borers.

Peat Moss

Peat is becoming an increasingly controversial subject. We are messing up great chunks of wild habitat in our craving for this soil amender. It has no nutritional value, so don't be fooled by professional gardeners who spread it around and suggest it is a fertilizer. It will soak up about 20 times its own weight in moisture and suck your garden dry if it is dug in without a good long soaking.

* I prefer to use coconut fiber as a soil amendment, but if you still use peat, be sure to give it a good soak before using.

PEAT POTS

Be careful with peat pots. A lot of plants are sold in them. They dry out rapidly and suck up water from all around. They do break down over a long period of time, but I usually remove them and cut them up for the compost.

* Soak plant and pot, slit the sides and bottom; cut off any parts above ground.

PENNYROYAL *Mentha pulegium*

This low-growing mint is supposed to ward off all sorts of pests, including ants and fleas, and make a good ground cover for the shade. If you can actually find the right plant, it might prove to be beneficial. If you happen to put in the wrong kind of mint through no fault of your own—more likely incorrect labelling—you can spend years pulling the stuff out. Try it in a small area, and if it really is pennyroyal it will hug the ground, and you can risk spreading it around.

PEONIES

Some of the most striking plants in my garden are the peonies. I love the single blooms and tend to prefer them to the big old-fashioned varieties. Even when the blooms are only a memory, the foliage remains a delight.

* The blooms will be larger if two side buds are removed. Keep well watered and plant in sun in well drained soil.

* For best results plant peonies in September. If you live in a very cold region or winter comes early, and you order by mail, prepare the holes well in advance

and store the soil where it won't freeze. Plant as soon as the shipment arrives, using the stored soil.

* Always plant peonies at exactly the same level as the pot. The eye should be no more than 2 inches below the surface. Too deep and they won't flower.

* Purple blotched leaves mean they are diseased. Cut leaves off and get rid of them.

* To create magnificent dried flowers, cut the blooms just as they are about to burst into full bloom. Hang upside down for a few weeks. They look like old silk; for best results dry the common, blowsy, heavy blooms, rather than singles or species peonies.

* Lay pine boughs over peonies to protect them from winter's ravages.

* There is a myth that ants are absolutely necessary to the opening of peony blossoms. Not true. They are attracted to the sap that the peonies exude when they are opening. They do not cause any harm.

PERENNIALS

After a garden has been converted from annuals to a mix of perennials, annuals, shrubs and vines, it will achieve marvellous new heights of beauty by the third growing season.

* Perennials should not be cut right back to the ground in fall. I usually leave either the whole stalk or a minimum of 8 in/20 cm of stalk, which adds extra protection by catching the snow and holding it. It also creates interesting winter shapes. Astilbes, sedums such as 'Autumn Joy', ligularias and hydrangeas left intact have ornamental seedheads that are interesting all winter.

* Divide early-blooming perennials in late summer or early fall; late-flowering varieties in early spring. I say this, but I seem to be dividing and moving plants all the time—except in serious heat waves or after a hard frost. With this method you take your chances, but it sure is fun.

* Invasive perennials can be kept in check by constant deadheading.

* To prolong blooming, don't cut spiky perennials back too early. And don't let them set seed or they won't flower again. Nip off the fading blooms but don't be disappointed that each successive bloom is smaller—just think of them as more exquisite.

PEST MANAGEMENT

Here are more ideas on how to get rid of pests in the garden:

* To attract insect-eating birds, introduce a bird bath into the garden; change the water regularly.

* Add a bat house to the garden. These animals eat huge numbers of night-time munchers and they sleep all day anyway.

* To keep worms off fruit:

> 1 cup/250 mL   vinegar
> 1 cup/250 mL   sugar
> 1 gal/4 L   (approx) water
> 1   banana peel

In a 1-gal/4 L plastic bottle, combine vinegar, sugar and water. Shake well; add the banana peel. Hang one open jug of this mess in each apple tree before blossoms open.

* Set traps in ice cream pails on the ground in rows between tomato plants or among raspberry and rhubarb plants to lure and trap insects.

* Sprinkle wood ash from the fireplace onto the soil around any plant that is susceptible to cutworms.

* Border any vegetable patch with annual catnip, which self-sows, for flea beetle control. You will, of course, attract every cat in the neighborhood as well. You have to decide which is the worst pest.

* Plant dill with any member of the cabbage family (brassicas).

* Tansy is an ant repellent. Plant it between rows of peas, cucumbers or cabbage to keep insects out.
* Sprinkle coffee grounds around the base of young vegetables to prevent root maggots.

See also INTEGRATED PEST MANAGEMENT.

PESTICIDES, COMMERCIAL BRANDS

To use noxious sprays, wear full-length pants and shirt and heavy gloves. Spray only on a dead still evening after bees have gone to roost. After using any pesticide, wash your hands thoroughly with detergent and cold water—not warm water, which will open up the pores and allow the pesticide to be absorbed into the skin.

* Commercial pesticides, no matter what any company says, have huge risks attached to them. I remember being completely turned off the cherries from one area. One slightly windy day, when I was visiting a nursery at the edge of a fruit farm, a man in

a moonsuit was going through the orchard spraying poison everywhere. We watched that green cloud coming toward us and headed out immediately. I could feel my tongue swelling and eyes closing and could taste that muck for hours. What that did to every insect in the neighborhood and how it affected the soil, one can only imagine.

* The more pesticides used, the more they need to be used, since insects build up resistance to them. It's a dangerous spiral. Use botanicals, natural products, integrated pest management and homemade recipes and you'll do the environment a great big favor.

PETUNIAS

The foliage of petunias is toxic to tobacco hornworm, Colorado potato beetle and some caterpillars. Make tea out of petunia leaves chopped up and steeped in boiling water, and spray on plants.

* Petunia leaves attract the very pests that they kill, which makes this a more valuable plant than I had imagined.

* Petunias protect beans against beetles.

* Try out the wonderful new petunias: 'Superfina mini' series and the fabulous 'wave' series.

----

pH

The acidity or alkalinity of your soil is something you should know about. Some plants will be miserable in an alkaline soil, others in an acid soil. On a scale of 1 to 14, 6.8 represents neutral soil, which is the ideal for most plants. The lower the number, the higher the acidity. It leaps as follows: 5 is 10 times more acidic than 6, 4 is 100 times more acidic than 6.

* To test the pH of your soil: Take 2 cups/500 mL of soil from three different parts of the garden at a depth of 8 in/20 cm. Mix these soils together. From the mixture take about 1 qt/1 L and send to your local agricultural station or college for testing. Ask to have any recommendations to correct an imbalance stated in organic, not chemical, terms.

* With great difficulty and over many years, you can change the nature of the soil in specific areas of your garden. If you must have rhododendrons and azaleas and have only neutral soil, you'll have to make it a bit more acid. First, make sure the area is wide enough to accommodate spreading root systems.

* Add pine needles, oak leaf mold and soaked sphagnum peat moss to make soil more acid.

* Add lime to alkaline soil to neutralize it.

* Scab disappears around pH 5, so no need to lime.

* Crops such as chicory, endive, shallots, sweet potatoes and watermelon grow well in soil with a low pH (an acid soil), so plant them in rotation.

PHENOLOGY

There are phenological traditions based on years and

years of noting the natural biological patterns or the timing of these processes in native or wild plants. Old-time gardeners used to watch their plants and calculate what they should be doing in any season, not by the calendar but by what the plants had to say.

* Two of the best *indicator plants*, as they are known, are lilac and honeysuckle. They are so widely available and so totally adapted to any given area where they grow that they can be counted on to perform pretty regularly. Some plants, of course, will try to rush the season because they are bigger, tougher and stronger. But these two are relatively reliable guides.

* Cool-season crops such as lettuce, peas and spinach can be sown when the lilac leafs out.

* Warm-season crops can be safely planted when the lilac blooms, since the plant is absolutely convinced that there's no danger of a further frost.

* Plant tomatoes, peppers and early corn when the purple lilac and the flowering dogwood are in full bloom.

* Plant squash and cucumbers when lilacs fade.

* This one comes from Montana: When the lilac blooms, alfalfa should be harvested to avoid alfalfa weevils.

* The best time to sow sweet corn is when the oak leaf is the size of a mouse's ear.

* Here's a variation from another part of the country: Plant corn seeds when the leaves of elm, maple and oak are about the size of a squirrel's ear.

* When the dandelion blooms, plant the kitchen garden: lettuce, spinach, beets and carrots.

* When apple blossoms are out, plant corn, cucumbers, pumpkins and squash.

* When daylilies start to bloom, set out tomato and pepper plants.

* There will be no hard frosts after the plum starts flowering or after the leafing out of aspen or chokecherry. Light frosts, however, may occur. Pansies, snapdragons and other hardy transplants can be put into the garden.

* When there is new growth on green ash, bur oak or grapes, it's time to plant out tender vines, perennials and annuals.

* Sow morning glory seeds outside when the maple leaf is full size.
* Plant early vegetables when the daffodils bloom.
* Plant potatoes when the shadbush, *Amelanchier canadensis*, flowers.
* There's another old saw that says when you can sit on the soil naked, you can plant. A bare hand will do just as well as a bare bottom.

Planting

After years of careful observation, you'll know when it's the right time to plant in your own garden. The rule that annuals must not be put out until May 24 is a rule that can be broken if you have a really protected garden that won't get hit by a surprise late frost. I have a protected downtown garden surrounded by large trees. My general zone is 6, but parts of my garden take plants that should grow only in zone 7. I tend to start planting shrubs and perennials by the middle of

April or early May. Sometimes I've been fooled—we often get our last snowfall April 21, but it doesn't really bother the plants as long as there isn't a deep, prolonged period of freezing. I continue planting into October. Hard frost doesn't hit my garden hard until mid- to late November. Each garden will have its own personal statistics like these.

* Always dig a bigger hole than seems necessary for the plant. Always wider than deeper. Water and see if the water drains away quickly enough to provide good drainage. If it doesn't, this means that the whole area has to be dug up and horticultural sand or grit added to the soil. To amend really poor soil, add compost and manure over a fairly wide area. I tend to add very little and concentrate on top dressing the plants. This allows the plants to settle immediately into the conditions they are going to face for the rest of their lives; then I add compost and manure to the surface of the soil. This means the soil is going to be fed and worms are going to work their way around the plants to pull in leaf mold, which will further break down and feed

the plant at its roots. When you see leaves being folded into the ground in spring, worms are working away for you. Water a plant well for the first few weeks until there's new growth and then reduce water specifically for the area and plant species. If I'm really worried about a plant, I'll keep it shaded for a few days.

* To create a new bed, I dig it up in autumn. Any cloddish pieces will be broken up by the action of snow and ice and not by back-breaking effort. Then, I lay down a deep thickness of compost, manure, leaf mold or any other organic matter that is available. In spring, this is now an easy area to work with and after a little bit of raking, you can get early seeds in.

* I always plant very, very early in the morning or late in the afternoon so that the plant doesn't have the stress of heavy-duty midday sun. It's cooler and more pleasurable at those times of day as well.

* For a straight planting row without using string and stakes, lay a long bamboo pole on the ground and press it into the soil. The impression makes a perfect planting guide.

* I think the following is a great way to recycle computer paper tailings. The perforated edges are perfect guidelines for planting seeds since the holes are ½ in/1.25 cm apart. Put the strip along a row and drop a seed in every hole, or every second, depending on how far apart you want the seeds. If it's recycled paper, just leave it in place and cover with soil.

* Plant tiny seeds, such as lettuce and carrots, by wetting a piece of cotton string, then dragging it through the seeds. They'll adhere to the string and you can place it right in the planting row. Cover with the specified amount of soil. Seeds will germinate at fairly regular intervals.

* Dig holes for fruit trees and shrubs in fall for spring planting. If the soil you've dug out is poor, amend it with compost, return to the hole and cover with boards so it won't compact over the winter. The soil will be lively and easy to work with in spring for a really early start.

See also DECIDUOUS TREES; PERENNIALS; SEEDS; TRANSPLANTING.

POISON IVY

If you garden at the cottage, it's a good idea to have a crash course on how to identify poison ivy—just saying three shiny green leaves is not good enough. Get a good picture of it and cruise the area, finding out where it is—covered head to foot and wearing stout boots. If you do get attacked by this stuff, rub either plantain or jewel-weed on it to soothe the skin. The remedy works for stinging nettle and raspberries as well.

* The above applies to poison oak as well. Some people get severe allergic reactions and should see a doctor immediately.

Poisonous Plants

You should know which plants are poisonous and which parts of which plants are poisonous. The most familiar is the castor oil plant, *Ricinus communis*, which has fatal seedpods. All parts of *Aconitum*, monkshood, are poisonous. Here are more to be wary of: *Aesculus*, horse chestnut; *Ailanthus*, tree-of-heaven; *Amaryllis belladonna*, belladonna lily; *Pulsatilla vulgaris*, pasque flower; *Arisaema triphyllum*, Jack-in-the-pulpit; *Asclepias* spp., milkweed; *Colchicum autumnale*, autumn crocus; *Convallaria majalis*, lily-of-the-valley; *Cypripedium* spp., lady's-slipper; *Datura* spp., angel's-trumpet; *Delphinium* spp., larkspur; *Digitalis purpurea*, foxglove; *Echium vulgare*, blueweed; *Euphorbia* spp., this family includes poinsettia; *Helleborus niger*, Christmas rose; *Hypericum perforatum*, St.-John's-wort; *Laburnum*; *Narcissus* spp.; *Nicotiana* spp., tobacco; *Ornithogalum*, star-of-Bethlehem; *Rheum rhabarbarum*, rhubarb—the leaves; *Rhododendron*—all parts, including the leaves; *Tanecetum vulgare*, common tansy; and *Wisteria*.

Poppies, Oriental

Poppy seedheads on these elegant plants are as decorative in bouquets as they are in the garden.

* The only time they should be transplanted is in September.

Potash

Potash, another word for potassium, is one of the major elements of plant life. Essential for the manufacture of sugar, it helps keep a plant disease-resistant and retain water, and protects it from cold.

* A plant is deficient in potash when the leaves get yellow streaks or spots on them, or they look withered.
* Add potash to your soil by applying manure, compost or granite dust, which will add potash slowly over a long period. Sheep manure has a higher potash content than other manures, so I tend to stick with it for everything.
* Chop up plants and leaves and dig them into the soil to add more potash.
* Wood ash is also a good source of potash, especially from hardwood. Use only on acid soils.

POTASSIUM

Like nitrogen and phosphorus, potassium is one of the essential elements. How to tell if you have potassium in your soil: the following plants will thrive— tansy, sunflower, marsh mallow, wormwood.

* If the soil is potassium-poor, red clover will grow easily.
* Add potassium to the soil by adding potash.
See also POTASH.

POTATOES

If you keep potato plants, cut back to about 10 in/25 cm of stalk. They will grow back quickly, and pests, such as **Colorado potato beetle**, will be discouraged, as will blight and other diseases.

* Plant an eggplant at each corner of the potato patch to attract Colorado potato beetle away from the potatoes.

* Planting beans with potatoes will give them some protection against this beetle while the potatoes protect the beans against Mexican bean beetle. A tasty combination.

* Plant horseradish near the potato path to fend off the potato beetle.

* Don't plant potatoes and tomatoes in the same area alternately, because they have many of the same diseases and pests.

* Dust the lower parts of potatoes with sulphur to lower the pH into the range of 4.8 to 5.4 and you'll find that scab is not a problem.

* Plant cabbages in between potatoes to give the former a good start.

* For quick rooting, start potatoes in sand before planting. Cut the potatoes in seed pieces, two eyes per piece, and lay them in large flats with 1½ in/4 cm of sand on the bottom. Jam the potato seed pieces

together and fill the flats with sand. Water and leave in a warm place. In two weeks potatoes will have sprouted and be ready for planting out. Do this before the last frost is expected, since the seeds will survive frosts but foliage won't.

* To produce tiny potatoes, which are marvellous for salads, squeeze them in tightly and use less space between rows.

* Potato slices can be used to discourage wireworms that infest root vegetables. Place slices near tomatoes, potatoes and cabbages. Make sure the eyes have been removed.

* Build a 4 by 4 ft/120 by 120 cm raised bed for potatoes. Plant them on the perimeter, then add another layer of wood and soil, repeat the process until you have a tower of potatoes.

* Divide potatoes into boilers and bakers by dissolving 1 tbsp/15 mL table salt in 1 gal/4 L water. Potatoes that float are best for boiling. Those that sink are for baking.

POTTING SOIL MIXTURES

A favorite: sifted soil plus screened compost. Solarize (sterilize) by putting the mix in a clear plastic bag and leaving it out in the sun. Allow to dry before storing. A few days before planting, wet the potting mix with a solution of 1 tbsp/15 mL bleach in 1 gal/4 L water.

* I think this is a delightful idea and wish I hadn't given my old crockpot away. In a crockpot, mix soil and compost, and heat slowly to get rid of pests such as ants. Start slowly so that you can pick out earthworms as they rise to the surface to escape the heat. This should take no more than two or three hours, unless you have a serious infestation.

POTTING UP

You usually must put rootbound plants into a pot the next size up. Some plants love to be rootbound, though, so make sure you know what you are doing.

* Partially fill the larger pot with potting mix. Set the smaller pot inside to create a mold, and then gently remove. Knock the plant out of its old pot and put it in the mold left by the smaller pot. This way you won't disturb the roots.

POWDERY MILDEW

This fungal disease can affect plants for a number of reasons: poor watering habits in spring; bad air circulation; the fungus overwinters in leaf litter that has been allowed to lie on the ground around the plant. Don't crowd plant or put susceptible plants (roses and phlox) in damp shade.

* Blend 10 cloves garlic in 1 qt/1 L water. Boil for 30 minutes, then strain. Cool to room temperature and apply as a spray at full strength.
* One tsp baking soda plus a few drops of soap in a pint of water.
See also DAMPING OFF; FUNGAL DISEASES.

Praying Mantis

A beneficial creature with a fierce look who feeds on soft-bodied insects such as aphids and leaf-hoppers. In August, they reach maturity and will cannibalize beetles, flies, spiders and tent caterpillars.

* You can introduce them into your garden by gathering them along roadsides. They are found in golden-rod clusters. Gather the egg cases with a section of twig and store in a fridge, or place them where you'll need them in the garden—they should survive very cold weather.

Pruning

This is one of the most important tasks for any gardener. How you prune will determine how good your garden looks.

* Use any ratty-looking old shrub to practice on and hone your skills.

* I used an old honeysuckle and started by cutting away no more than one-third of the shrub each year, including all the dead stuff, crossed branches and anything awkward. I practiced which way I wanted branches to grow: point outward to grow out, inward to grow in—new sprouts will follow the direction of the cut and help to hide it. The placement of the bud on the stem below the cut establishes the direction of the new branch. An outside bud will produce an outside branch.

* When I take secateurs out into the garden, I wipe them off with a mild solution of 1 part bleach to 9 parts water as a disinfectant. It's very easy to

move a disease around the garden on the blades of a cutting implement.

* Observe your plants. Shrubs don't have to be pruned each year. Shrubs that bloom in mid-summer or later can be pruned in spring. Spring-flowering shrubs can be pruned immediately after blooming. The only rule is to prune so that you can't tell it has been touched.

You can safely prune after a plant has finished blooming, or to take out old twisted or dead growth.

* Never use any sort of wound healer. Each plant has its own defenses and it's best not to interfere with them.

* Never, ever cut into the cambium (the first layer of bark) on a tree. Cut back only to the collar, where the branch and trunk are attached. And never cut *into* the branch collar, which is the tree's zone of protection.

Never make a flush cut on a tree or shrub. This will wound the tree immeasurably.

* When pruning is done properly, a ring of callus forms around the cut, protecting the wound, the first season and will decrease the amount of sprouting on the tree.

* Prune most trees late in the dormant season to cause as little injury to the tree as possible.

* Start early and you can train any tree or shrub to the shape you want.

PYRETHRUM *Chrysanthemum coccineum*

Look for this ingredient on any commercial insecticide you buy. The dried flowers are considered safe by ecological gardeners and it breaks down easily in sunlight.

* Plant it in your garden to help plants fight off ticks.

QUACK GRASS *Agropyron repens*

Easy growth of this weed indicates a shallow hardpan. It can be removed by planting millet, soybeans or cowpeas. Two crops of rye will also get rid of it.

* If it's in your grass, make a brine of table salt and apply to the weed after cutting the grass. This is difficult to keep from going elsewhere so dig out the quack grass and sow clover in its place.

Rabbits

These animals may be cute, but they are a scourge in some areas.

* Mesh or wire fences dug deeply into the ground—at least 1 ft/30 cm—and only 2 ft/60 cm high will keep them out of a vegetable patch. Just as long as the top is floppy. Plant anything to distract them—clover, grasses, even their own patch of carrots.

* If this doesn't appeal, try dusting plants with talcum powder or scatter blood meal around.

* Dust ashes or cayenne pepper around to keep these adorable little monsters out of the vegetable patch.

* They hate onions, so by planting onions throughout the garden, you may discourage them.

* Mark your territory with pee. See Deer.

Raccoons

I live on an ancient raccoon path, and these guys spend a lot of time generally whooping it up at night. Raccoons like to search for grubs, which makes them not all bad for the gardener, but they may also take out new plants at the same time. I scatter cayenne pepper around to keep them out of specific parts of the garden.

* If you have a vegetable garden, especially corn, try the following: Plant a wide swath of squash around the corn patch to keep them out. Squash flourishes in the shade of corn (they both like raised beds as well) and raccoons hate squash.

* I think this is a riot: Tape the corn to the stalk so that they can't get it off. Do this just before it ripens, which is when the raccoons like to do their noshing.

* Add a layer of chicken wire to the top of any fencing and it won't hold the weight of the animal.

* If you have a pond and want to discourage them without putting in an electric fence, float a large glass ball in it.

* Make sure your pond is raised high enough and deep enough so that they won't bother your fish: 2 ft/ 60 cm is a minimum. Have vertical sides so they have nothing to lean on.

RAGWEED *Ambrosia* spp.

This is the plant that really affects allergy sufferers, not goldenrod. It produces an unbelievable amount of pollen—as much as several million grains per plant— which spreads easily on the slightest breeze, and will drift as high as the seventh floor of an apartment building.

Because it is wind-driven pollen, the blossoms don't have to attract pollinators. As a result, they are innocuous and almost the same green as the foliage. Goldenrod, on the other hand, has brilliant yellow blossoms. If you spot ragweed, which has fern-like leaves up to 15 ft/5 m high, keep mowing it or pulling it out. Don't ever let it get near the seed stage.

Rain Butts

Everything old is new again in gardening. I remember these from my childhood on the prairies when not a drop of water was ever wasted. Now it's easy enough to have a plastic garbage pail on a small (18 in/45 cm square) dolly under a downspout. When the pail is full, wheel it to the garden and set another pail on the dolly ready for the next deluge. This relay system will ensure that you always have fresh water.

* Make sure it has a well-fitted lid or you may find squirrel corpses in there. Not pleasant.

* Go to any place that manufactures Chinese food. Soya barrels are cheap and cheerful in color, and hold gallons of water.

Raised Beds

Raised beds drain very effectively, but they dry out quickly. They are terrific for starting seeds or improving really terrible soil. They are a boon to the handicapped or arthritic gardener.

* If you want to get rid of an area of grass, make a raised bed with the sod you cut out. Turn it green side down, cover with manure to help the composting process, and soon you'll have a tidy raised bed.

* In each of the following cases, the material turns into finished compost and is a rich source of nutrition for plants.

* Prepare beds with 1 ft/30 cm high edging, fill with manure and soak thoroughly. Let sit until it has shrunk, leaving about a 4 to 6 in/10 to 15 cm depth on which to put topsoil. If you cover it with heavy dark plastic, it will solarize (heat will kill off any weed seeds).

* Combine manure with semifinished compost that's been screened, and top up with soil.

* Bedrock, rocky soil or a steep hill all need raised beds. Try this marvellous trick: Put bales of hay on top of the bed in a single layer. Wrap the sides with plastic to hold in water. Leave each bale intact (they should last about three years). Sprinkle compost inoculant over the bales to help start the process. Make a hole in the hay and insert plant or seed along with a handful of soil. Water well. In the first year stay with transplants or large seeds. By the second year you won't need anything and the bales will have rotted sufficiently to maintain even fine seeds. Sprinkle soil or a soil mix on top just to cover. This method is from a great book called *Garden Smarts* by Shelley Goldbloom.

Raspberries

In August, make T-shaped posts and tie in new canes while they are flexible. Cut out the old ones. Allow 9 canes per yard/10 per meter to develop. Pull out the rest. Get rid of suckers; and remember that weeds leach out water from the ground. Summer-fruiting canes can be pruned once finished; fall-fruiting canes can be cut to ground in late fall or early winter. Or remove only the fruited tips. The remaining canes should fruit again in June.

Rats

If you are wary of composting because it might attract rats, don't worry. Use good composting techniques and rats probably won't be interested in your pile. Rats are more likely to be attracted to restaurants and other places where food is left out for garbage and the pickings are really easy.

* If you should happen to sight a rat anywhere near your compost, line the composter with hardware cloth. This stuff is great—it has 1 in/2.5 cm square holes, is malleable and easy to cut with garden clippers. Make a container to go within the composter

with a wire top that can be easily lifted up and propped open.

* I've found that by not putting *anything* with protein in the compost, rats have never bothered with mine. No meat, eggs or leftovers with butter.

* Get rid of any rats' nests you might come across and make sure there is no handy source of food nearby. Put garbage only in a container that shuts tight and put it out on the day it's going to be picked up.

RHODODENDRONS

Rhodos are a great favorite, and people want to grow them whether or not their gardens have the right conditions. The smaller and darker the leaf, the more exposure to sunlight is tolerated; the bigger the leaf, the more shade it needs. You can determine the eventual size by the length of stem between last year's and this year's blossoms. If it's short, it will be a relatively slow growing, small shrub. If the stems are long (up to 1 ft/30 cm or more), it will be a rapid-growing, tall shrub.

* If rhodo leaves are wilting but getting enough water, they are probably suffering from:
a) Root rot—too much water in winter, or b) Excess weevil grub damage.

* If a plant has gone chlorotic, use a foliar spray of 1 tbsp of Epsom Salts and 1 pint water. It should green up in a week.

* Don't put rhodos near the side of the house where winter winds come howling past. This is a woodland plant which must have dappled light, wind protection and, most important, protection from sun scald in March.

* In early spring, when the leaves are not on the trees, tie Christmas tree branches on the south side of the plant.

* Plant them surrounded by other plants, rather than exposed as specimens. Woodland plants like the company of evergreens and other trees. Duplicate their original conditions as much as possible. They are shallow feeders, so plant them just at the surface or on a small rise of soil.

* Few insects bug them—one exception is the root weevil. Make a collar of cardboard and place on the surface of the soil around the trunk. Apply Tanglefoot to the cardboard and these night crawlers will get stuck and die. Apply nematodes for the grubs that do most of the damage.

* Never apply any fertilizer containing aluminum sulphate. Rhodies are light feeders and this stuff is toxic to them.

RHUBARB

The leaves of rhubarb are poisonous, so they make a good spray for vegetables. Boil rhubarb leaves in water;

dilute the solution by one half. Before sowing brassicas and other vegetables, spray the soil with this tea.

* Use rhubarb spray on roses to protect them against greenfly and black spot.

* To get longer, more tender rhubarb stalks, make a ring of wooden stakes around plant. Secure black or green plastic garbage bags around outside of stakes and leave open at the top.

ROAD NOISE

The only way to baffle road noise is to plant a large dense hedge. In fact, put in a double hedge—a lower one on the outside and a higher one inside. See HEDGES.

RODENTS

Plant *Fritillaria imperialis*, crown imperial, around

the garden. It has a skunky odor and will keep squirrels, mice and other rodents from any bed it grows in. Don't, whatever you do, keep this in the fridge. If you do, *everything* in the fridge will stink.

* Ro-pel is a spray that may keep animals away from your plants. It doesn't work for everyone but I know one gardener who sprays her shrubs and trees with it. She identifies each one with a white ribbon as she goes along, and it keeps deer away.

* She cuts back her perennials, and consequently, voles tend to bother her garden less. See also DEER.

ROOT CUTTINGS

To increase your stock, take pieces of root from houseplants and perennials in late winter. For best results, start them in compost and soil in a cold frame. Most plants will come true to the parent.

* Don't bother to take cuttings from variegated

plants, however, since they seldom come true. Variegation is often an anomaly.

ROOTING HORMONES

Create your own rooting hormone: Crush fresh willow branches in a shallow pan; cover with water. Let sit for 24 hours. Soak 1 to 2 in/2.5 to 5 cm of cutting in the extract overnight at room temperature.

ROOTING SUCCULENTS

Some of my most beloved and useful plants are in the succulent category. Sedums, for example, can fill almost any role in borders or pots. They are also the easiest plants to start from cuttings. Just snip off a piece with a fairly long stem, stick it into soil, and within a few days it will have taken root.

Roses

I've always hated the sight of a bunch of tea roses standing stolidly in rows with brightly colored heads and naked legs. They need company. Grow dianthus around them—the two go together beautifully. Make a collection of dianthus as well as roses, blending and contrasting the colors of each variety of plant. If dianthus isn't your taste, try a benign runner, such as *Lathyrus*, the perennial sweet pea. I have one growing up a *Rosa glauca*; it blooms when the rose is building gorgeous red hips.

* Place banana skins just below the surface of the soil. They contain calcium, magnesium, sulphur, phosphates, sodium and silica—all necessary trace minerals for a rose's health.

* I always plant a clove of garlic beside my rose bushes. Garlic gives off a toxin from the roots that keeps greenfly and aphids away from the plant. Garlic is also said to make the scent of the flowers more powerful.

* Cut roses last longer if you slice the stem on a sharp

angle and peel away the last couple of inches/centimeters. Then submerge the whole stem in hot water. When the water has cooled, transfer flowers to a vase with cold water. This method also revives drooping roses.

* Epsom Salts supply magnesium to the soil, so add at least 1 tbsp/15 mL to the base of rose bushes in May and then again in June, to encourage new growth.

* Add leftover tea leaves to the soil around roses—they respond well to tannic acid.

* In midsummer, put a handful of alfalfa sprouts around the base of each rose bush to give it a good feeding.

* Plant parsley to get rid of rose beetles.

* If you're worried about Japanese beetle, dust with milky spore disease or plant white geraniums (zonal pelargoniums) nearby.

* Make an infusion of elderberry leaves and warm water; spray to get rid of caterpillars.

* Roses should be pruned when new growth appears in the spring. Hybrid tea roses are pruned 6 to 10 in/

15 to 25 cm in height with five to six canes per plant. Each cane should have two to three outward-facing buds.

* In early winter after the ground is frozen, prune for the last time. Cut the canes to 3 ft/1 m high to lower the chance of them being whipped about by winter winds.

* To promote more flowers on climbing roses, train the canes to grow horizontally.

* If it's possible, place roses so that they get at least six hours of sun—preferably in the morning so that dew dries quickly, preventing fungal diseases. Never sprinkle water over roses—always water them from below.

ROTENONE

Rotenone is a botanical derived from tropical plants. It's the product of last resort for most ecological gardeners.

ROTTING

Rotting of fruits and vegetables can be prevented if you train them up a trellis. Try it with cantaloupe, cucumbers, midget watermelon and some squash. The trellis can be vertical or horizontal.

* Make a platform: Cut up pieces of wood large enough to support the ripening fruit. Set the fruit on top of the wood to keep it high and dry.

ROW COVERS

These are plastic or horticultural cloth draped over semi-circular forms to protect rows of seedlings, usually vegetables, from marauding pests looking for a free meal or a place to lay their eggs. They allow air and light to reach the plants, and are put in place during periods of risk and removed once the danger is over.

RUE *Ruta graveolens*

Plant near roses and among vegetables to ward off Japanese beetle. Keep away from herbs such as basil—the basil loses every time. Some people react badly (almost like a reaction to poison ivy) to rue, be careful when you are handling the plant.

* Cats tend to steer clear of rue, so make an infusion and spray precious furniture or anything else that a cat may damage.

Sabadilla

Powder from the seed of this Caribbean plant is considered one of the botanicals. About ⅔ cup/150 mL powder makes 1 gal/4 L spray.

Sage *Salvia officinalis*

One of the most useful and beautiful of all herbs, no garden should be without sage. The flowers form on old wood, so don't chop back *Salvia officinalis*, common garden sage. In early spring, the tricolored and purple forms of sage can safely be chopped back.
* Grow with carrots to protect against the carrot fly. Don't plant with cucumber. Brassicas are helped by having sage as a companion.

* Make a tea with sage and pour it over plants for a healthy hit.
* Sprinkle dried sage over kitty litter to keep the smell at bay.
* Wormwood inhibits the growth of sage.
* Sage is a marvellous pot plant for the winter. Cut back about one-third and harden it off by bringing it slowly into the house. Make sure it gets lots of sun, and don't overwater.
* Sage is hardy to Zone 3, so it can over-winter in the garden.

SANDY SOIL

Rainwater will go through sandy soil at the rate of 20 in/50 cm per hour or faster. Water chemically extracts aluminum and iron from surface layers and deposits it in the subsoil, turning it red, leaving the top bone white with silica.

* To amend sandy soil, add large amounts of humus in the form of leaf mold, compost or well-rotted manure. If you use peat moss, be sure to add it when wet. See PEAT MOSS.

SANTOLINA
Chamaecyparissus, lavender cotton

Another of my all-time favorite plants—magnificent when used to edge a knot garden or any other border. Improve the silver foliage by clipping after it flowers (kind of a boring little yellow thing).

* A good moth repellent.

* Fill a container with this plant and move it around the garden wherever you need silvery gray.

SEA SALT

Use a line of salt as a dead line to keep some soft-bodied pests out of a special area. It has to be renewed after each rain. Careful, though, don't get it near unaffected plants.

SEAWEED

Seaweed has micronutrients that may be missing from other fertilizers and is known to contain growth hormones resulting in excellent plant growth and development.

* The great beauty of seaweed is that it doesn't contain any seeds, insect eggs or plant diseases. It breaks down easily and releases potassium and trace elements quickly.

* It prevents legginess in seedlings when mixed with soil and makes plants more disease- and insect-resistant. Seaweed makes an excellent foliar spray. However,

timing is essential. Spray tomatoes and other vegetables when you transplant, just before the blooms open, and as the fruit starts to develop. If you spray every two weeks until blooms open, color will be brighter.

* This natural fertilizer contains quantities of nitrogen, phosphorus and potassium that will change depending on type and the season. It has trace minerals as well as potassium chloride, common salt, sodium carbonate, boron and iodine.

* Since seaweed contains nitrogen and phosphorus, it will speed up compost activity.

* If you live near the sea, use it as a mulch or put it in the compost. But check first to make sure this is not prohibited.

* Seaweed may give tomatoes and citrus fruit some resistance to frost. It gives beets essential boron.

* Use a seaweed solution to speed up germination of seeds.

* Cabbage worms hate seaweed.

* Use a seaweed drench to get rid of root maggot

infestations. Soak seaweed in an equal amount of water for 24 hours.

SEEDLINGS

If seedlings get leggy, cut off the tops and put the latter in jars of water. Set out both at the same time to extend the number of plants you have. The water-rooted ones will mature later.

* Thin seedlings when the leaves touch. Snip off extra seedlings; don't pull them out or you'll disturb the roots of others.

* To encourage better root development in a leggy transplant, lay it sideways. It will develop a root system along the length of the stem.

* Presoaking flower seeds in warm water doesn't guarantee results, but try this trick: Put them in a yogurt maker or bundle them up and leave to soak in a thermos of warm water overnight. Good seeds swell up.

* Always water seedlings with warm water that has been sitting for a minimum of 20 minutes to get rid of most of the chemicals in tap water. Cold water will lower soil temperature significantly for hours.

* Put seeds in recycled containers with holes in the bottom for drainage, and set them on an old mirror slightly angled to catch the rays of the sun.

* To boost the intensity of the light reaching windowsill seedlings, surround them with foil-covered cardboard sheets or other shiny material.

See also SOWING SEEDS.

SEEDLING PLANTERS

Recycle plastic cutlery by using the handles as plant labels.

* A cheap alternative: Presoak cardboard egg cartons, fill to three quarters and scatter seeds on top.

* Use meat (or fish or chicken) trays from the supermarket as seedling planters. Cut along one side and

tape two together to create a long narrow pocket. Fill with soil. Remove the tape when the seedlings have developed enough and plant in place. See also SOWING SEEDS.

SEEDLING PROTECTION

To protect seedlings set outdoors for the first time, use old 250 mL milk cartons. Open the top completely. Cut down each corner to the shoulder of the carton to form four rectangular flaps. Turn the carton over and cut the bottom from corner to corner, following the X to form four triangular flaps. Lower the carton, top end first, over the plant. Mound up enough soil to hold each flap in place. If a frost threatens, simply push the triangular flaps

down to close the carton and hold in place with a flat stone. Reopen once danger of frost has passed.

* Another easy method: Take a 2 qt/2 L plastic pop bottle and cut off the bottom 2 in/5 cm; use this as a tray to start seeds. Place bottle over seedlings as a mini greenhouse. Remove the screw tops for ventilation.

Seeds

Soak seeds with hard coats such as peas, beans, corn, asparagus, morning glory, nasturtium, lupines and sweet peas for 12 hours in de-oxygenated water—boil for five minutes to eliminate gasses, place in an air-tight container, and cool. Water with de-oxygenated water to stimulate root branching.

* Store seeds in the freezer. This makes them viable up to 10 times longer than storage in any other manner. Make sure they are completely dry. Store in a moisture-proof container—add a bit of milk powder to absorb any excess moisture. If the seeds are moist,

they will expand with freezing and burst the cell walls.

* To test the viability of seeds, try this: Small seeds should break rather than bend, large seeds should shatter when struck with a hammer rather than mash up.

* When you're given what seems confusing leeway as to how deep to plant seeds, what you are being told is that the depth is determined by soil quality. The heavier the soil, the shallower the depth; plant deeper in sandy soil.

* Here's an old tried and true method that always works for me: Never plant a seed deeper than four times its diameter.

* Presoaking seeds can be more reliable if you put them in an empty tea bag and let them hang in a thermos of warm water overnight.

SERVICEBERRY *Amelanchier canadensis*

One of the best plants for bird habitat as well as being

the perfect screening plant. Grows to 21 ft/3 m and has white flowers in spring, edible berries in summer and blazing autumn color. Grows in shade.

SHADE

Shade is a plus in any garden. It provides protection from the sun and is infused with a sense of calm and coolness.

* If you don't have a shady glen, create one by planting trees and shrubs. Think in terms of layers—big trees protecting smaller trees protecting shrubs and so on down through the large perennials to the carpeting on the forest floor.

* If you have a small garden, try a shady corner on a very small scale. Though your palette will consist mainly of greens, yellows and whites, variegated plants will add a sunny note.

* Some shade plants that I grow in my own woodland area: *Kirengeshoma palmata*; *Astilboides tabularis*;

Clethra alnifolia; many broadleaf evergreens such as rhododendrons, azaleas; *Pieris japonica*; *Kalmia*, mountain laurel. Architectural stunners such as *Petasites japonicus*, elephant ears; *Darmera peltatum*, umbrella plant, both of which can be invasive in moist shade; perennials such as *Thalictrum*, meadow rue; *Aruncus*, goat's beard; *Anemone japonica*, Japanese anemone; any *Aquilegia*, columbine; *Dicentra*, bleeding heart; *Amsonia tabernaemontana*, Willow blue-star.

* Ground covers: *Lamiastrum*, archangel; *Lamium*, dead nettle; *Pulmonaria*, lungwort; *Galium odoratum*, sweet woodruff; *Asarum europaeum*, European ginger. And, of course, the kings and queens of the shade garden, hostas—green, blue, yellow and many variegated forms. Collect them. See HOSTAS.

* Herbs for the shade: mints; *Myrrhis odorata*, sweet cicely; *Angelica*; tarragon and chervil.

* Consider shade when you are planting companions in the vegetable and flower borders. Tall plants can act as shady protectors for small, low-growing plants.

For instance, lettuce between cabbages, broccoli and tomatoes. The lettuce can be harvested before the bigger slower-growing plants.

* Shade areas under shallow rooting trees, such as beech and maple, are difficult. Try raised beds and shallow-rooting plants, or mulches such as shredded pine bark, cocobean hulls or pine needles.

SHRUBS

To plant shrubs properly, dig a hole that is the same depth as the root system and about five times wider. Don't amend the soil and don't backfill with amended soil. Once the roots move out of amended soil, the shrub is subject to enormous stress.

* Soak the newly planted shrub thoroughly with a slowly dripping hose. A deep soaking,

which might take hours, encourages deep roots and saves worrying about watering needs for a few weeks. They need lots of water the first year and can probably get along on rain water thereafter. See also DECIDUOUS TREES; PLANTING.

SLUGS

Slugs provide food for birds, which is about the only good thing I know about them. Nothing enrages me more than to see the damage wreaked by these creepy crawly slimers. They are the one pest that I go after assiduously in my own garden. I'm told that if you pick 300 a day you can clear up your garden in three years. I've been at it for 35 years and I'm not sure I've made a dent. However, there's something quite exhilarating about stomping all over these repulsive creatures at the beginning and end of the day. I don't mind holding a handful of them, but it takes practice not to be totally revolted. I go out at night with a flashlight, now that I've trained the neighbors not to be terrified, and get a great crop.

* Never put poison on slugs because birds eat them, and you'll bump off your local bird population.

* The smaller the slug, the more devastating its destruction.

* Slugs are great predictors of rain. Before rain, they come out in the hundreds for easy picking. Or so I've observed.

* Sprinkle coffee grounds around areas that slugs favor.

* To control slugs, try this recipe from a Rodale publication. It's cheaper than putting out beer for these ingrates:

> 1 tbsp/15 mL brewer's yeast
> 1 tbsp/15 mL honey OR molasses
> 1 tbsp/15 mL cooking oil
> 1½ cups/375 mL water

In a 2 cup/500 mL plastic container, combine yeast, honey OR molasses, oil and water. Place in the soil

with the top at ground level. Replace every few days and right after rain. Be sure to empty every morning.
* Here's a variation. Slugs are attracted to the fermenting mixture.

```
   2 tbsp/25 mL  sugar
     ½ tsp/2 mL  baking yeast
 2 cups/500 mL  water
```

Combine sugar, yeast and water. Dig a shallow depression in soil and set saucers or other containers into the soil with the top edges flush with the surface. Pour ½ cup/125 mL into each saucer.
* A good brew to discourage them is tea made with the chopped leaves of *Artemisia absinthium*, wormwood. Pour hot water over the leaves, strain, and cool. Pour the infusion around plants to kill any slugs that have gone underground, especially in the fall.
* Crush egg shells in a food processor; sprinkle around the garden in spring.

* Epsom Salts spread around vegetables such as lettuce and cabbage keeps slugs away.

* Well-soaked clay pots or pieces of wood set among plants provide a nice dark place for slugs to hang out during the day. But it still means you have to go around scooping them up and killing them. Be cruel and plop them into Bacillus thuringiensis or salt. It will dry them out but it's a slow, agonizing death.

* Horseradish leaves attract slugs—and you'll make a good early-morning catch. Put a few leaves in areas where they gather. Use them to lure slugs out of the soil in spring.

* Use copper strips to encase beds of vegetables that are particularly vulnerable to slugs.

* Make a line of salt or lime around new plants attacked by slugs (once you've got rid of the ones inside the line).

* Take a cookie tin or plastic container 7½ in/19 cm square by 2¾ in/7 cm deep. Cut out three oval-shaped flaps in the lid measuring approximately 2 in/5 cm wide and 3 in/7.5 cm long, positioning cuts so that the

flaps start at the edge of the lid and are an equal distance apart. Put lid back on tin and fold the flaps downward to within ¾ in/2 cm of the bottom. The flaps act as ramps for the slugs to go down, but since they don't reach the bottom, the slugs can't get out. Set into the ground so the rim is barely above ground. Prepare the following concoction:

  1½ cups/375 mL corn syrup
    1 tbsp/15 mL lemon juice
    1 tbsp/15mL grape jelly
   2 cups/500 mL water

Combine corn syrup, lemon juice, grape jelly and water, and bring to a boil. Stir until jelly and sugar are dissolved. Pour mixture into tin. Change the solution every three weeks.

Snapdragons

Snip off the top half when the plant is 4 in/10 cm tall and stick the cutting in the ground to root. The original plant will grow fuller. Cut back every 10 to 14 days to keep them flowering.

Sod

Recycle sod to repair worn or damaged spots in the lawn: remove damaged turf, aerate the soil, and press new sod into the empty place. Water well until established. See also Berms.

Soil

Soil, an incredible material, comes in a huge range of profiles. It's important to understand how it works. Reading about it will help, but working with it is the best teacher of all. I've found over the past several years that leaving the soil alone, not disturbing it by cultivating, but putting compost and manure or other soil amenders and fertilizers on top, has left my soil in magnificent condition. This, in spite of the poor conditions under which I garden—shallow-rooted trees everywhere. Think of the life beneath your feet, all those small creatures from worms to bacteria to nematodes and how they get disturbed when you dig around in their farms. I call this laissez-faire gardening. Let nature do what nature's supposed to do, and do what you have to do to be a good steward of the soil.

* Here are the elements that soils must have: oxygen, silicon, aluminum, iron, calcium, magnesium, potassium and sodium in decreasing volume. Trace elements are also important. The texture of the soil is due to the size of the mineral particles. There are a few main soil types:

* Heavy clay soil: Holds its shape when wet.

* Sandy soil: Doesn't hold its shape when wet, and the

drainage is fast, sometimes too fast for plants to grab the nutrients they need.

* Silty soil: Powdery; doesn't crumble; but it has lots of minerals in it.

* The proportion of sand, silt and clay determines what kind of soil you have.

* If there is too much clay, soil will be dry, hard to work with; however, it is still chock-a-block with nutrients. Don't despair if you have it. Add lots of compost, leaf mold and manure to the surface and the soil will slowly become more friable.

* If there is so much sand that the drainage is way too swift for most plants, add compost to the surface to encourage earthworms. These, in turn, will make the soil more moisture-retentive, because their bodies produce a slime that helps all the little particles in the soil adhere to each other.

Solarizing

Solarizing the soil kills off all sorts of unwanted weeds and their seeds. In fall, spread black plastic over the ground you want to purify; make sure all the edges are held down by bricks or stones. It will heat up in the early spring, and the soil should be weed-free in a few weeks.

Sowing Seeds

The rule of thumb is to sow seeds at a depth equal to four times the diameter of the seed.

* Always sow seeds when the moon is waxing, not waning. During this period the air is filled with moisture that will help germination.

* Sow very fine seeds evenly by mixing a packet of seeds with a few tablespoons/milliliters of clean white sand or fine coffee grounds. Spread the mixture over the soil or prepared container.

* Quantity:

> One for the mouse,
> One for the crow,
> One to rot
> And one to grow.

SPIDER MITES

Crops, with the exception of cole crops, are vulnerable to spider mites. Any plant that's been sprayed with insecticides, unless it was also a miticide, will develop infestations. Watch the lowest plant leaves and look for stippling: small yellow dots or red spots on top of leaf, underneath red, brown and orange, or pale yellow with black side spots.

* Try the following for houseplants: Wash the leaves and stems with a mild dish detergent and room-temperature water. Borrow a cigarette or buy cheap pouch tobacco, crinkle it up and put it around the

base of houseplants. The tobacco kills off overwintering spider mites. Don't overdo it.

* Bud mites stunt leaves; russet mites can turn tomato plants into bronzed dead foliage overnight. Dust with sulphur, which also controls powdery mildew. Make sure you apply it so that the dust billows upwards through the plant. (Don't apply to melons and squash.)

* An old method is flour-paste spray that sticks to the mites. Make a gravy-like mix and spray on the affected plant.

* Apparently, predatory mites live on cattail pollen in spring, then feed on pest mites during the summer. Get some cattail pollen and transfer the predatory mites onto plants that need them. These predatory mites take on the color of their prey, are the same size as the pest, but don't make webs. The pest mites have side spots and are rounder. Lacewings, ladybugs, bigeyed bugs, pirate bugs, damsel bugs, dance flies and thrips will eat spider mites.

Spring-Blooming Plants

These plants should not be lifted or moved until after the flowers are finished. Fall-blooming plants can be safely transplanted in spring.

Squash

Plant a few radishes in each hill of squash to ward off insects. Nasturtiums also repel squash bugs.

Squirrels

Squirrels drive most gardeners I know absolutely crazy.

* Here's an idea from *National Gardening Magazine*: Take old leather belts and drive 4 in/10 cm finishing nails into the leather every 4 in/10 cm; wind the belts around tree trunks from lower part of the trunk into

the branches. Don't do this if you have kids or animals who might climb the trees.

* I managed to keep squirrels out of windowboxes by using a collection of seashells as a mulch—very irritating for the squirrels; looked pretty as well.

* Another traditional way of keeping squirrels at bay is to lay down chicken wire or mesh around plants and over bulb beds. Their toes get stuck in the wire. You can make wire baskets and set your bulbs in them. I tried what I thought would be really annoying—spreading plastic wire netting over a bulb bed. The squirrels managed to figure out how to get under it and dig away.

* Soak bulbs in Critter Ridder or Ro-Pel before planting to make them smell and taste horrible.

* Finally, always plant bulb delicacies, such as tulips, with some narcissus, which are poisonous to the squirrels.

* One friend swears that by giving them peanuts, corn and peanut butter they leave them alone.

* Besides narcissus, which squirrels hate, equally repellant are hyacinths and muscari. Mix these in with tulips and crocus.

STARTER SOLUTION

Seaweed extract and fish emulsion make splendid starter solution that helps young plants recover quickly from the shock of transplanting:

> ½ cup/125 mL fish emulsion
> ½ cup/125 mL seaweed extract

Mix ingredients and pour into a jar. Seal tightly. Store in a cool, dark place. To use, add 3 tbsp/50 mL solution to 1 gal/4 L water.

* Use for foliar feeding as well.

STERILIZING

Sterilize soil when you are preparing your own container mix or starting seeds.

* To sterilize a flat of soil, drench it with boiling water. It will take about 1 gal/4 L for a normal size flat.

* Sterilize containers by soaking in a solution of 1 part chlorine bleach to 10 parts water.

* Sterilize containers by immersing them in boiling water or baking in a 180°F/85°C oven for 20 minutes before using.

* Use an old electric frying pan. Combine garden soil with sand or vermiculite or peat; place 1 cup/250 mL water in frying pan and fill to the top with potting mixture. Cover, and turn to low. After half an hour, test the temperature with a soil thermometer. When it reaches between 150 and 160°F/65 and 70°C, unplug the pan and let cool to room temperature. This is better than stinking up your oven, and it can be done at an outdoor plug.

STINGING NETTLE

No gardener wants to have a garden full of weeds, but this one could prove to be the exception. It makes neighboring plants more resistant to slugs, lice and snails during damp periods. It bumps up the aromatic herbs such as angelica, marjoram, mint, sage and valerian.

* Nettle strengthens the growth of tomatoes.
* Make a fermented extract spray from nettle to repel slugs and snails. Allow the herb to steep in water for three weeks, strain and store.
* A solution of nettle added to the compost speeds up decomposition.
* Vegetables keep in storage much longer when they are planted near nettle.

STRAWBERRIES

If you add some forest duff (the organic matter) from below spruce or pine trees when you plant, and then mulch with the needles, you'll produce more flavorful fruit.

* Combine strawberries with bush beans, spinach and borage for added flavor. Pyrethrum planted nearby helps ward off pesky insects.

* Mulch with pine needles and straw, alone or together.

* Use an everbearing strawberry plant for a child's garden. Flowers and fruit grow all through the season and it spreads easily.

* Plant strawberries beneath roses as a delicious ground cover.

SUGAR

To reduce the amount of sugar you need in recipes by one half, add lemon balm, sweet cicely or angelica.

Chop up sweet cicely and add to strawberries with a touch of sugar.

Sunflowers *Helianthus* spp.

One of the craziest sights I've ever seen was a group of fruit trees each with a sunflower planted alongside. This was like putting up a flag saying "Eat me." If there's one flower birds and squirrels will go after, it's the sunflower.

* Use them as a windbreak if you have the space, and they are certainly large enough to screen out a part of the garden. I think they are just right for a children's garden—a fast-growing, entertaining plant.

Sun Scald

My hortgurus who have rhododendrons keep their Christmas trees and tie the branches on the south side of vulnerable shrubs. This protects them against the scalding sun in March when so many rhodos and broadleaf evergreens are susceptible to damage. We keep forgetting that there are no leaves around to shade them.

* Make a tent of burlap for rhododendrons: Drive four stakes into the ground in the shape of a square about 4 ft/1.2 m from the trunk, or far enough away from the limbs that leaves aren't brushing the edges. Make sure the stakes are firmly anchored in the ground. Wrap burlap around the stakes, holding it in place with staples or tacks. Don't interfere with the shallow, delicate root system. If you plunge the stakes into the ground too close to the plant, you'll hurt the root system; too far away and the wind will whip the leaves around anyway. Repeat for three or four years, until the plant is acclimatized.

* To protect young bark from sun scald:

> 1 tsp/5 mL flax soap or other pure mild soap
> 1 cup/250 mL hot water
> ¼ lb/125 g diatomaceous earth

In a bucket, dissolve soap in hot water. Wearing a mask, carefully add diatomaceous earth to make a slurry. Paint this muck on tree trunks from the soil line to the first branch.

TANGLEFOOT

A commercial insect killer considered okay for the organically correct garden.

* Cover rubber balls with plastic wrap sprayed with Tanglefoot; hang them around the garden. They will pick up all sorts of flying insects that attack plants. At the end of the season get rid of the outside wrap and store the rubber balls for the winter.

TANSY *Tanacetum vulgare*

Tansy, an old-fashioned herb that escaped from gardens generations ago, has naturalized all along railway embankments and in ditches. I brought my seeds carefully from Culpeppers in England, raised them myself, and now it's everywhere. Be careful where you plant it. It's hardy, though invasive, but extremely useful for the ecological gardener.

* It's almost as good in the compost as stinging nettle because it's rich in potassium.

* Tansy keeps cabbageworm, cabbage butterfly, flies, ants, Japanese beetles, striped cucumber beetles and squash bugs away from most crops.

* I plant it near my doors to keep ants out and it works. Rub it into your pet's fur to keep off fleas.

* Tansy planted under fruit trees helps repel borers that invade the fruit, especially peaches.

* An excellent companion for roses and raspberries—it makes them produce prolifically.

* Tansy dries fairly well and looks good in large bouquets with grasses and wild plants such as Queen Anne's lace.

* I have a slight skin reaction when I handle tansy.

Tarpaulins

Use an old tarp or thick sheet of plastic rather than a wheelbarrow to drag around heavy bags of fertilizer, manure or peat moss. They are also useful for hauling rocks. Rake leaves onto a plastic tarp before putting them in bags to rot.

Tarragon *Artemisia dracunculus*

For cooking, make sure you buy *Artemisia dracunculus*, French tarragon. There are other plants, such as Russian tarragon, that are boring, invasive and not particularly flavorful.

* Divide every three years in spring by taking a section of root and easing it away from the clump.

TERMITES

To kill off these pests, cut off the source of moisture that keeps them going by using Silica aerogel, which will desiccate anything it touches.

THYME

Every garden has a place for thyme. My own bed of thyme includes the following: *Thymus richardii*, a good shrubby plant excellent as an edger; *T. citriodorus*; *T. alpina*, both white and pink forms; *T. vulgaris*, commonly used in cooking; *T. serpyllum*, Mother of thyme; *T. pseudolanuginosus*, woolly thyme; *T. montanus*. For a tapestry of thyme, add any others that you can find.

* Plant with eggplant, tomatoes and potatoes to increase their health.

* Reportedly repels cabbage worms and whiteflies.

TOADS

If you can lure a toad into your garden, it will consume insects by the hundreds. Cutworms, grubs, rose beetles, caterpillars, ants, sow bugs, moths, mosquitoes and flies are just a few that are food for a toad. They are land creatures and need water just like any other animal so ensure they have a constant supply. They must have a cool place to hide in or escape from local cats. I have a beautiful clay toad house, but, alas, no toad. An upside-down clay pot will do as well. Don't worry about them in winter. They bury themselves in the ground and hibernate.

TOBOGGANS

Use a toboggan or plastic snow carpet to drag heavy shrubs about as you plant in spring.

TOMATOES

Even in the tiniest garden it's possible to grow tomatoes. Grow them on balconies, in pots, or in rows as a fence around a vegetable garden. And they will keep growing in the same place for years unless the soil becomes infected by a disease. They are heavy feeders, so give them lots of compost and manure.

* Always water tomatoes deeply at the bottom of the plant. Use warm or tepid water. They are sensitive creatures.

* If you are a smoker, always wash your hands before handling these plants.

* Don't plant near corn or potatoes.

* Sweet 100 tomatoes will come back from seed and be just as tasty.

* Hybrids are generally sterile, but a tomato that self-seeds may revert back to a tasty parent and you might get lucky.

* Make sure there is bone meal in your starter mix to

give tomato seedlings enough phosphorus. If they turn purple, you know they lack it.

* Make tomato cages out of hardware cloth or concrete-reinforcing wire. Once the tomatoes are finished, put the cages over your other raised beds, like a Quonset hut.

* Drape cages in plastic mesh to discourage cabbage moths and bugs. Cover with old screens to give extra shade.

* Make 4 in/10 cm long collars from ⅛ in/3 mm PVC drainage tubing to protect plants from cutworms. Or cut up plastic bottles so that you can put them over the seedlings. Push the mouth end into the soil.

* Make plant protectors for seedling tomatoes out of black roofing paper. Cut strips of paper about 1 ft/ 30 cm wide; wrap one around the base of each tomato cage. If you stake tomatoes, circle the plant, stake with paper and hold in place with a few small sticks in the ground. The black paper captures heat and prevents wind damage, which compounds transplant shock. Leave in place until plants are growing vigorously. I'm

told it increases production by half.

* Another form of plant protector: Cut #9 wire into 5 ft/ 1.5 m lengths and bend into hoops. Stick the hoops into the soil just over 1 yard/1 meter apart; drape a sheet of 4 ft/1.2 m wide 1.5 mil plastic over the hoops; weigh down the edges with rocks or soil.

* If tomato seedlings are exposed to a slight breeze, even from a fan, for an hour a day there is a definite reduction in growth rate.

* Wrap the bottom of tomato cages with heavy duty plastic. Plant the seedlings and set out the cages early. By the time the seedlings have reached past the protection of the plastic, they will be flourishing.

* To grow early tomatoes, expose young transplants to 55°F/13°C temperatures at night for three weeks once leaves have unfolded. This will produce sturdier plants, stronger side shoots and earlier growth than those grown indoors.

* Plant tomatoes near asparagus and they will repel the loathsome asparagus beetle, as well as cabbage worms and cabbage butterfly from cole crops.

* Plant near gooseberries to guard against insects.

* Companion plants for tomatoes: Chives, onion, parsley, marigolds, nasturtiums and carrots. And roses—to ward off black spot; this may look a bit odd as a piece of garden design.

* Process tomato leaves in a food processor, add 1 qt/1 L water and 1 tbsp/15 mL cornstarch. Mix, and use as a foliar spray. Works well against whitefly on houseplants.

* Plant borage among tomatoes to attract bees and help set fruit early.

* Leggy transplants may result from starting seeds too early. When this happens, bury the plant so that the entire stem is under the soil and only the top foliage is exposed. The tomato will root along the length of the stem and you'll get a stronger root system.

* Blossom end rot is

a thick leathery brown/black lesion or sunken area on the bottom of tomato fruits. It's caused by stress from calcium deficiency, infrequent watering or cultivating too close to the plant. Add lime, which is an excellent source of calcium, to the soil before transplanting. Mulch and always hand weed.

* Withholding water during the maturation stage hastens ripening.

* Another trick to speed up ripening is to plunge a border spade into the soil in a circle around the plant. By limiting how far the root system spreads, you will make the plant concentrate on setting fruit.

* Train tomato plants up trellises on south-facing walls (they must have at least six to seven hours of sun a day). Make sure they aren't under the eaves or they will be in rain shadow and subject to serious drought.

* If frost threatens tomato plants while they are still loaded with partly ripe fruit, cover them with blankets at night. Reduce watering to help fruit ripen faster. Or put a plastic tent over the plants at night.

* Keep frost-threatened plants going another month

by spreading a thick layer of straw or shredded news-paper around them. Remove stakes and lay the plants on the mulch as far as possible without breaking them. Cover with plastic row covers.

* If there are still green tomatoes on vines in late fall, take up the whole plant and hang upside down in a dark, airy, cool place with a box just under-neath. The fruit will ripen naturally and plop into the box.

Tools

Garden tools should be kept clean. They can be the primary agent for spreading diseases around the gar-den. To keep them clean, put 3 tbsp/50 mL household bleach into 1 gal/4 L water. Wash them off regularly with this solution.

* Keep them sharp with a flat, oiled whetstone. Wipe with linseed oil to prevent rust.

* Invest in a wire brush to remove stubborn dried

mud from shovels and spades. Then sharpen the blade with a file held at a slight angle away from the blade. This will make it easier to cut through sod and roots.

TRANSPLANTING

The best time to transplant is on a cloudy or a slightly rainy day, in the late afternoon or at other times when things begin to cool down.

* If you must transplant when it's out of season or too cold, puddle the plants in warm, not hot, water.

* Give transplants a hit of fish emulsion food before setting them into the garden.

* To help transplants re-establish quickly, gently loosen roots and spread them in all directions.

* To make a really neat transplanting hole, use a cleaned-up putty knife. Cut a square around the transplant and you'll get a good plug of soil without disturbing roots.

* To transplant a major tree or shrub, start a year ahead and cut a circle all around the dripline. This will prune the longest roots and force the plant to form shorter ones near the trunk. A year later there will be much less damage when you move the tree or shrub.
* Recycle yogurt containers by cutting off the bottom and punching holes in the lid. Turn the containers upside down, fill with potting mix and plant seeds. Just unsnap the lid when you want to transplant and push the whole thing—soil and seedlings—into the planting hole. Or use old coffee cans that have plastic lids. Cut off both ends of the can, punch holes in the plastic lid; plant seeds and wait until the first few leaves are showing. Dig holes large enough to accommodate the can, push into planting hole and lift can out.

TREE BORERS

Discourage them by making a thin paste of wood ash and water; paint it on trunks. Control these pests by making sure your tree has enough water and compost. Don't prune when the adults are laying their eggs because they'll get into the wounds.

TREE TIES

Discarded bicycle inner tubes cut into 1 ft/30 cm lengths make good ties. Twist into a figure eight with one loop around the tree, the other around the supporting stake.

* Good old pantyhose are also useful.

TREES

The method of planting trees has changed as we understand more about the structure of trees. Instead of digging a deep hole and filling it up with amended soil, dig a hole that's the same depth as the root system and about five times as wide. Spread the roots out in all directions because this is the way they'll grow. If the soil is amended, the tree is set up for future shock. When the roots grow past the good stuff into alien territory, they'll be in for a period of stress.

* I've never tried the following, but you could experiment on a small tree transplanted from one spot to another. Put a quart/liter of oats or other grain in the bottom of the hole and away from the roots. As the grain ferments and composts, it creates heat that helps the roots grow.

* If you are worried about the health of a specific tree—it doesn't seem to be doing terribly well—take soil from around a tree of the same species that is doing well and dig it in around the problem tree. There might be something in the soil that will give it life.

* Compacting the earth around trees harms feeder roots.

* Use as much original soil as possible when transplanting trees and shrubs. There are some beneficial fungi in the soil that will help reduce the shock of transplanting.

* Trees are crucial as wildlife habitats.
* Always check to see what nature's doing, and try to emulate it.

See also DECIDUOUS TREES; PLANTING.

TRELLIS

I am prejudiced when it comes to trellis. I think that the opening should be a minimum of 4 in/10 cm to make a graceful square-opening trellis. The ideal is about 1 ft/ 30 cm squares framed within a handsome fence.

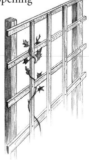

* Trellis as trompe l'oeil: Make a small space look much larger by having trellis work disappear into the horizon. For ideas, look at books on old trellis ornamentation. Trellis works well on a small deck or balcony.

* One of the nicest tunnels I've seen used commercial trellis behind a swimming pool. Roses and clematis climbed over the surface consisting of the large metal hoops and sheets of trellis. At the end of the tunnel, there was a lovely bench in its own private space.

* If you have a large country property (or know someone who does), start collecting appropriate lengths of sticks to form a rustic trellis out of natural forms.

* Use trellis inside the garden to provide natural enclosures and garden rooms. I have a pretty square trellis screen that cuts off the sight of the compost and provides a mid-garden work station. Once the shrubs and vines grow up over it (a slow process in the shade) it will be almost hidden. This is a great way to screen out garbage areas, air-conditioning units or children's play areas.

* When attaching trellis work on any wall, make sure there is at least 2 in/5 cm of space between wall and screen.

* You can make cheap, almost invisible, trellis out of hardware cloth. This 1 in/2.5 cm square metal is easy to cut to size. Hang the cloth on L-shaped screws at the top. Hold the cloth flat along the sides with these screws. See also VINES.

TULIPS

I don't know why but species tulips seem to be scorned by squirrels in my neighborhood. I've given up buying all others. The little ones (2 to 12 in/5 to 30 cm) don't seem to interest them. Species tulips also tend to multiply and return more dependably than the taller varieties. Look for tulips recommended for rock gardens; and species tulips: *Tulipa greigii*; *T. kaufmanniana* and *T. fosterana*.

* Plant tulips in buried plastic berry baskets 9 in/23 cm by 12 in/30 cm by 4 in/10 cm deep to keep them away from rodents. After flowering, dig up the whole

basket and move them to an out-of-the-way spot. Fill in the hole with annuals. In fall, move the tulips back to your favorite spot.

* Plant or sow annuals all around bulbs to detract from decaying leaves. Use the same color as the bulb to keep a color scheme going and to remind you in fall what lies below.

See also Bulbs.

URBAN FOREST

The urban forest is one of our best protectors against pollution. Since almost 70 percent of our urban forest is on private property, property owners must be good stewards. Trees scrub the filthy air of our cities, and the more trees we plant, the better the atmosphere. They may be our only hope of being able to breathe properly. A city tree is far more efficient at converting carbon dioxide into oxygen, even more so than a forest tree. In spite of this, there is an attitude that trees are dirty (leaves) and require too much work (leaves). Yet leaves are the greatest bonus we have as gardeners. In their leaves trees hold the nutrients we need to grow healthy plants. It's like putting sunlight back into the soil.

* They help rainwater to percolate through the soil thus charging groundwater supplies.

* Trees modify the climate by drawing water from deep in the soil and transpiring it, which reduces temperatures during the day and keeps nighttime temperatures more even.

* In my own small space I've planted 20 trees and almost 150 shrubs. The only time I feel healthy is when I'm working around them. We work in harmony together, and that's probably why I'm so exhilarated when working in the garden.

* When planting trees in the city make sure that the species you choose fits the site. Do you want a graceful canopy? What about overhead wires and street lights? How close are they to motor traffic and sidewalks? Every region has native species that do extremely well. Here are suggestions for trees that can stand up to city pollution:

* *Ginkgo biloba*, ginkgo tree, is not only one of the oldest, most beautiful trees on the planet, it has the most benign root system of all. You can plant safely under the tree, and it stands up to pollution beautifully. *Platanus acerifolia*, London plane; *Gleditsia*,

honey locust; *Carpinus betulus*, European hornbeam; *Corylus colurna*, Turkish filbert; *Amelanchier*, service-berry; *Cornus kousa*, Japanese dogwood.

* Salt tolerant: *Acer campestre*, hedge maple; *A. pseudoplatanus*, sycamore maple; *Caragana arborescens*, Siberian pea shrub; *Robinia pseudoacacia*, black locust.

Dry sites: *Ulmus parvifolia*, Chinese elm.

Wet sites: *Alnus glutinosa*, European alder; *Quercus bicolor*, swamp white oak; *Taxodium distichum*, bald cypress.

* For small gardens: *Cercis canadensis*, eastern redbud; *Cercidiphyllum japonicum*, Katsura tree; *Celtis occidentalis*, hackberry.

VACUUM CLEANER

One of those wet/dry numbers can be useful in the garden when the garden is dry. Try vacuuming insects off plants such as beans, peppers, tomatoes and strawberries if your garden is badly infested.

* Dump vacuum cleaner detritus into the compost—it's biodegradable.

VALERIAN
Valeriana officinalis

This herb adds phosphorus
to the soil.
* Earthworms are attracted to
it, so add this plant to the compost
for increased activity.

* Valerian is available in different forms at most health food stores. It has a calming effect on people, cats, dogs and even rats.

VERTICAL VEGETABLES

Cucumbers grown on a fence or trellis grow straighter than those allowed to ramble along the ground.

* I have a neighbor who makes slings for her melons. She grows them along fences and up poles. When the fruit starts to come along she fashions slings around them. The bigger and heavier they get, the more the sling—rather than the vine—supports the fruit. In a tiny back garden she reaps an enormous harvest.

* Scarlet runner beans are not only good to eat, the brilliant flowers are beautiful and they are a superb instant screen or coverup.

Vine Borers

At the first sign of wilting in long runners or if you see little piles of greeny yellow sawdust, borers may be attacking the base of the plant. Once inside the plant, insecticides are useless.

* Start with row covers, then dust if you must. Rotenone is a botanical substance derived from tropical plants, and though it kills off larvae, it also upsets the ecology of a garden. Don't use it unless you have to.

* Inject Bacillus thuringiensis into the plants if borers have already entered the stems. It's easier to take a razor blade, open the stem where the attack occurs, and remove the borer. Cover the cut with moistened soil.

* If you've had an infestation, take up the old vines, get rid of them and forestall a second generation.

VINES

Sometimes we're so anxious for instant results from the beds in a garden that it's possible to forget about tending to the walls. That's why I always advise people that the first thing they should consider putting into the garden is the vines they want. Many vines take several years to really become established.

* If you're trying to teach a vine to climb and it's having trouble getting started, take some strips of old pantyhose (the lighter the color the better), tie them to a trellis, porch or wall and start your plants up these. Somehow they seem to grab on to this more quickly than conventional trellising. The right color will disappear into the background and eventually the material will disintegrate and disappear.

* Prune vines by taking out all the dead stuff in spring.

* Prune some clematis such as *Clematis jackmanii* back to about 1 ft/30 cm from the ground.

* For instant covering with vines, put in annual seeds

between perennial vines. Plant morning glories, scarlet runner beans or lablab, also known as hyacinth bean.

* If you have a very ordinary evergreen and want to tart it up, allow a small flowered species clematis to grow up the branches.

WALNUTS

Black walnut trees secrete a toxin, juglone, from their leaves and roots. It causes nearby plants to wilt. Plant susceptible crops—broccoli, brussels sprouts, cabbage, cauliflower, eggplant, peas, peppers and potatoes—as far away as possible.

* English walnut, *Juglans regia*, doesn't have leaf and root excretions but does create dense shade; keep that in mind when you are planting. Try some of the shade-loving herbs such as angelica, mint and sweet anise at the foot of this lovely tree.

WATER

The quality of water you pour over your plants will affect them profoundly. Most of our tap water is filled with chemicals, and plants will either succumb or adjust. If you are hand watering, make sure you let the water sit for a good 20 minutes to allow chemicals to evaporate. It's good practice generally to water with tepid, rather than really cold, water, especially when you are dealing with seeds, seedlings and transplants.

* Save water from cooking vegetables. When cool, use it to water houseplants in winter and containers in summer.

*With the fear of West Nile virus being carried by mosquitoes hatching in standing water, empty pools and bird baths regularly.

Water Gardens

Water gardening is still only part of my fantasy life, but I've talked to enough watergarden experts to understand what the common mistakes are.

* Most people make their water gardens and ponds far too small and regret it almost immediately.

Make sure you have a minimum of 25 sq ft/2.3 m² of water surface.

* Form an outline of the planned shape with light-colored rope or hose, or even lime on a very still day. View it from every possible angle including any part of the house from which it will be seen. Live with this for a few days until you have confirmed the proposed shape.

* Figure out what you're going to do with all the displaced soil. Books merrily tell you to remove all this stuff, but what do you do with it? Spread the topsoil to other parts of the garden or put it to one side. Use the subsoil as the underpinnings of either a berm (see BERMS) or perhaps a waterfall. Move the topsoil back into place and plant, or use the soil to create raised beds in other parts of the garden.

* Be sure that the pond is at least 2 ft/60 cm below

grade in zone 6 areas and deeper the farther north you live. Therefore, the hardy plants you choose can be moved in their pots to the center or deepest part of the pond over the winter. Even plants designated as hardy should be given some care. They cannot spend the winter exposed or frozen. If you can't for some reason leave them in the pond, bury them in the garden.

* Cut back deciduous hardy plants in autumn, give a good soaking and store indoors in garbage bags so they won't dry out. Or if your pond is deep enough, simply move the pots to the center. Tropical waterlilies must be stored indoors.

* Most plants are oxygenators, that is, they take in carbon dioxide and give out oxygen, so you have only to be judicious in your choice of plants rather than be guided by plants that are designated as official "oxygenators." People tend to expect too much of these plants. Bullrushes and cattails—two different species and not to be confused—are the most effective plants for cleaning water.

* If you have an explosion of algae, just skim it off

with a rough piece of wood. Never siphon out the water to start again; you'll just give the algae more to feed on. Water, when left alone, will restore itself. If you have some algae, this is a good sign; it means there's no runoff from nitrates that might exist in the garden. Clean pond water is not necessarily clear water. If you can see your hand 1 ft/30 cm below the surface, you have clean water.

* Always have the water at least one-third in the shade—provided by the large leaves of such plants as waterlilies.

* Use three small plants or one large plant for every square yard/square meter of water surface. Some water plants are great spreaders, so do be careful and read labels.

* Use heavy clay gardening soil when you pot up water plants. Any light commercial medium will simply dissipate.

* I love the look of ornamental grasses by any water garden, pond, waterfall or even swimming pool. The verticals are reflected in the water and make a dramatic

contrast with the strong horizontal levels. *Scirpus*, bull-rush, comes with dark green, blue, white or zebra-striped foliage; *Typha*, cattail, has the dark brown poker familiar in drainage ditches everywhere. *Colocasia*, taro, is a tropical with green or dark red leaves; *Sagittaria*, arrowhead, can have single or double white flowers. *Glyceria maxima variegatus*, manna grass; sedges (any of the *Carex* varieties) also love wet soil or shallow water.

WATERING

Watering is one of the most important aspects of gardening. Your plants won't survive without some watering. To use water wisely and efficiently is becoming increasingly significant. This precious resource is not always readily available and we're probably all going to be on meters someday.

* Soaker hoses are pretty good. Some are constructed of recycled tires that leak the water out slowly in a capillary action so that it runs down and across roots. No water is lost to evaporation, but in some spots it crosses paths—and why water paths?

* Here's a suggestion: Slide old bicycle inner tubes around any sections crossing paths. Bury the tubes on each side and the water will dribble into the beds and leave paths dry.

* Make your own drip irrigation system by punching holes in the bottom and sides of large coffee cans. Bury a can in the midst of a vulnerable group of plants, or what will potentially be a thirsty group, before sowing seeds. Once they've hit the cotyledon stage, switch from surface sprinkling to deep irrigation by filling the cans with water. You can also add manure or compost tea this way. Water will get to where it's needed—the roots—more quickly.

* One of the most valuable acts you can perform for perennials, roses, shrubs and trees is to water them deeply before they go into dormancy in the fall. This will help them cope with the coming days of drought.

Do this before there is threat of hard frost.

* Be sure to water trees well beyond the leaf canopy where there are tons of feeder roots.

* One of the most delightful chores of the garden is handwatering. I have a great old watering can with a long handle so it's easy to lug 2 gal/8 L around at a time. I spot the plants that need help by watching the indicator plants in the area—when the indicator plants look droopy, I concentrate on that area. Watering under the leaves and close to the stems means that you aren't splashing mud around that might affect the health of a plant. And you get to know your plants well when you water this way.

* Drill a hole in a plastic 1 gal/4 L jug and place it at the base of a tomato plant. Refill about twice a week so that water seeps in at the roots. The rest of the plant will stay dry and so will spaces between rows, thereby cutting down on weeds.

* Give especially thirsty plants a drink by sinking clay pots in the ground nearby and filling them with water.

* Watering houseplants when you're away for a few days: If your bathroom has some natural light, set a dishrack upside down in the bathtub with a few inches of water in it and set pots on top. Poke the end of a shoelace into the soil through the drainage hole far enough up so that the lace touches the soil. Let the other end dangle in the water.

* To water both seedlings and indoor plants: Use plastic talcum powder bottles with adjustable tops. Squeeze fine spray over seedlings or onto the foliage of plants to clean them.

* Put a rain barrel or other form of rain butt under the downspout closest to the garden and attach a soaker hose to the lower section of the barrel. Run the hose through flower beds. As the rain accumulates in the barrel, it will flow gently out to the flowers.

WATERLILIES

These delicate but gorgeous plants are tropical varieties and will have to be wintered over in most parts of the country, unfortunately. But it's relatively easy to leave them in a container with damp sand. The temperature should be about 55°F/12°C.

* In spring, start tubers indoors by floating them in water at about 75°F/24°C.

Webworms

These pesky little bugs love fruit and nut trees. Their ability to make webs sometimes confuses people into thinking they are tent caterpillars. Spray with Bacillus thuringiensis.

* Introduce trichogramma wasps into the garden. They are the webworm's natural enemy.

Weeds

Weeds are not always the enemies we make them out

to be. They perform valuable functions in nature, and I'm not one who thinks a garden is dirty or unkempt if it has a few weeds in it. Weeds grow for a reason—they rush in to take advantage of any open site for survival, but they also protect exposed topsoil. Without them, many open spaces would be ruined by sun, rain and wind. Of course, animals that eat them and defecate are adding to the nutrients in the soil as well.

* As soon as they appear, cultivate weeds, don't wait until they are firmly rooted. Even better, mulch, mulch, mulch. It's best to weed after a good rain, when the soil is soft and roots are less likely to resist. Throw any weeds without seeds into the compost—they are full of nutrients, including valuable trace minerals.

* Any weed with a long tap root such as **Queen Anne's lace** or dandelion goes deep down into the soil and brings up minerals.

Once the plant is cut off or turned under, these minerals feed the soil near the surface.

* Cut off the tops of weeds and let them lay fallow in rows and along paths. They will break down quickly into compost.

* Weeds as conditioners. Weeds have fibrous root systems that, when allowed to decay, add humus to the soil. They leave channels that earthworms can travel through. The channels also aerate the soil. Any soil that grows lots of weeds will grow lots of vegetables.

* Use weeds as indicators rather than as a discouraging element. (See next page.)

* Smother weeds in the lawn with grass seed. We used to repeat "In with the good seed, out with the bad weeds" when we had grass. Or try clover.

* Rake in some compost on the lawn, and sprinkle grass seed on top just before it rains.

WEEDS, AS SOIL INDICATORS

Many weeds are high in elements lacking in the soil and become excellent indicators of what kind of soil you have. By turning them under you add the missing ingredient.

* Poor soil will support such deep-rooted weeds as ragweed, mullein, Queen Anne's lace, mugwort and dandelions. A lawn covered in dandelions is probably lacking in calcium. But dandelions also serve a purpose, so I wouldn't want to remove all of them from my garden. Digging out the roots helps aerate the soil and of course you can always eat the young plants. By amending your soil and helping it become more fertile, you help get rid of weeds and you won't need herbicides.

* **Chicory**, a wonderful cornflower blue plant, grows in soil with a high lime content. Pink flowers on chicory indicates the soil is acidic.

* Acid soil is indicated by daisies, docks, hawkweed, horsetail, knapweed, Eastern bracken, silvery cinquefoil, hop and rabbit foot clover, horehound, knotweed, mullein, wild radish, garden sorrel and wild strawberries.

* Alkaline soil is indicated by mustard, most thistles, chamomile, wild carrot and creeping bellflowers.

* Hardpan is indicated by chamomile, field mustard, horse nettle, morning glory, pennycress and pineapple weed.

* Heavy clay soil is indicated by creeping buttercup, chicory, coltsfoot, dandelion, broad-leaved dock and mayweed.

* Light sandy soil is indicated by bindweed, goldenrod, sheep sorrel and corn spurrey.

* Low nitrogen is indicated by clover, vetch, rape and black medick.

* Poorly drained or waterlogged soil supports colts-

foot, Joe-Pye weed, sedges, smartweed, creeping buttercup, hedge nettle, horsetail and silverweed.

* Humus-rich soil will have lamb's quarters, chickweed, chicory, common groundsel, henbit.

* Shallow-rooted weeds, just in case you need to know this, will grow in more fertile soil: chickweed, chicory, common groundsel, horehound and lamb's quarters. If they appear after you've amended the soil by adding humus and compost, it means your poor soil is improving.

Weeds, How to Suppress

Weed retardant mulch: If you have a leaf shredder, run old newspapers through it along with the leaves—it will add volume to the leaf mulch. If you know someone with a paper shredder who doesn't know what to do with all that shredded paper, you can recycle it this way.

* Weed killer: Mix 1 lb/500 g of ordinary road or table salt to 1 gal/4 L of boiling water. The hot brine kills just about everything you pour it on, so be careful.

* This is an excellent way of getting rid of weeds between bricks or cracks: Pour on boiling water on its own or mix 1 tbsp/15 mL salt in 2 qt/2 L boiling water.

* Plant buckwheat between wide rows of vegetables and around vine crops to edge out competing weeds. It grows quickly.

* Discourage perennial weeds by allowing them to grow until just about to flower, and then mow them down. Leave the cuttings in place to mulch or throw the detritus into the compost.

* Creeping weeds: quack grass, Bermuda grass and bindweed. Once they are 4 to 6 in/10 to 15 cm tall, cut off at soil level; don't pull on them—you will make the situation worse. Eventually this practice will weaken the root systems and help their demise.

* Bulbous weeds: nut sedge, Bermuda buttercup. When bulbs send up new growth, pull out just before flowering.

* It's the simple weeds that grow long tap roots—curly dock, dandelion and chicory. Weaken plant by constantly cutting back the leaves and stalk. If you dig and leave anything behind, each piece can send up new shoots.

WEEPING FIG *Ficus benjamina*

If your weeping fig is shedding too much, mist the plant daily with cooled chamomile tea. Not only will the leaves stop dropping, they'll end up shiny and bright.

WHISKY BARRELS

Whisky barrels cut in half have traditionally been used as planters. But though they are very good, they're large and bulky and almost impossible to move once filled.

* They are, however, terrifically useful for anyone living with a balcony or roof garden. To lighten the load, use plastic containers placed upside down in the bottom third. Fill in the spaces between with plastic packing popcorn; then add soil.

* The very same barrels make great rain butts. Reposition a downspout so that rain water is directed into the barrel. Start a cress garden in it.

Whitefly

This insect attacks inside the house or greenhouse when there's a deficiency of phosphorus or magnesium in the soil. Hang squares of shirt cardboard painted with Tanglefoot or any other yellow sticky substance to get rid of them.

Windbreaks

Consider planting windbreaks first for a large urban or country property, especially ones by the sea or on a hilltop. Establish the direction of the prevailing winds; plan a windbreak around the following elements:

* In the country or on the prairies, windbreaks or shelterbelts should be 20 to 75 ft/6 to 23 m from the house in the path of the prevailing winds, and planted closely. For a shelterbelt, use larger trees in the center tapering down to smaller trees and hedges. Use a double line of deciduous and evergreen trees and shrubs for winter protection.

* Among the beauties good for prairie shelterbelts; *Acer negundo*, box elder; *Amelanchier alnifolia*, Saskatoon berry; *Caragana arborescens*, Siberian pea tree; *Celtis occidentalis*, hackberry; *Elaeagnus angustifolia*, Russian olive; *Syringa* spp., lilac; *Salix alba*, white willow. Evergreen: *Picea glauca*, white spruce; *Picea*

pungens, Colorado spruce; *Pinus ponderosa*, western yellow pine.

* Windbreaks also reduce evaporation; the moist air increases yields as far away as 50 ft/15 m.

WINDOWBOXES.
See CONTAINER GARDENING

WINTER DAMAGE

One of the saddest moments in the garden year is when you go out in spring and survey winter damage. Freeze-thaws, sun scald and just plain cold can be devastating to woody plants. Herbaceous plants suffer mainly during freeze-thaw cycles when they are heaved out of the ground. They are safely dormant the rest of the time.

* Pantyhose cut into 3 in/7.5 cm strips and wound

round a vulnerable tree trunk in fall will protect it from damage. The same works for the trunks of low-lying shrubs.

* A great deal of winter damage can be warded off by good mulching practices and by leaving most plants with their stalks intact during the fall cleanup. Carefully placing plants helps too. Grow vines on fences, place woody or evergreen plants beneath them, and you'll protect the roots. The vines in turn will cut down on the winds that go ripping through the garden. See MULCH.

WINTER GARDENS

Any gardener wants a garden that is as interesting in winter as the rest of the year. If there is a blanket of snow, my garden looks ethereal. With just a little care and thought, it can be one of the most beautiful times of year. Plan the bones of the garden around its appearance in winter by planting hedges and evergreens in a pattern or an axis that will stand out against the snow.

* Place ornaments so they can be viewed easily against the snow. A stone bench, which is useful in summer, is sculptural when there is a fine dusting of snow on it. Position statuary, objets d'art, even collectibles, so that they draw the eye out into the garden. I rearrange the garden for winter by moving all my favorite totems and sacred objects to spaces that will become empty when plants disappear.

* Here are a few of my favorite plants for the winter garden, no matter what its size: Evergreen shrubs, such as *Juniperus* spp., juniper; *Pieris japonica*, Japanese andromeda; *Andromeda polifolia*; *Taxus cuspidata*, yew; **Mahonia**, Oregon grape; rhododendrons such as 'PJM' and *R. impeditum*, both hardy types; *Chamaecyperis filifera aurea*, a golden yellow; *Hamamelis*, witch-hazel, good for scent

and bloom in late winter; *Aucuba japonica*, Japanese laurel, zone 7 and warmer; *Ilex crenata*, Japanese holly; and *I. verticillata*, winterberry, which is one of North America's hardiest native deciduous hollies. Its virtue is an abundance of scarlet berries that provide food for birds.

* Ground covers: *Hedera helix*, English ivy, *H. h.* 'Baltica', Baltic ivy; both good for zone 6 and warmer; *Paxistima*, rat stripper; *Vinca minor*, myrtle; *Pachysandra terminalis*, spurge; *Juniperus horizontalis*, creeping juniper; *Cotoneaster dammeri*.

* Shrubs with bright-colored twigs: *Kerria japonica* (green); *Cornus alba* 'Sibirica' (red).

* Trees with magnificent bark: *Prunus subhirtella*, flowering cherry; *Quercus palustris*, pin oak; *Acer negundo*, box elder; and in zones 6 and warmer the great *Acer palmatum* 'Sangokaku', coralbark maple, which has scarlet bark in winter.

* Evergreen perennials: *Polystichum acrostichoides*, Christmas fern; *Helleborus foetidus*; *H. niger*, Christmas rose; *H. orientalis*, lenten rose; *Asarum euro-*

paeum, European ginger; *Bergenia cordifolia*; *Erica carnea*, winter heath, blooms in February; *Calluna*, heather; *Arum italicum*, Italian arum; *Cyclamen*; *Yucca filamentosa*.

* Ornamental grasses: *Festuca ovina* 'Glauca', blue fescue grass; *Miscanthus sinensis* 'Gracillimus'; Maiden grass.

* Vines: *Celastrus scandens*, bittersweet, which has brilliant orange berries; *Pyracantha coccinea*, firethorn, great red to orange berries.

WIREWORMS

In spring, these pests do most of their damage. Adult beetles, "click" beetles, overwinter, then hatch eggs in spring. Generation overlaps make this a real annoyance. Cultivation exposes all stages of this pest to weather and enemies.

* Make a trap by

putting half a potato cut side down about every yard/meter. Wireworms will burrow inside. Digging up the vegetable patch in fall exposes them to their enemies.

WISTERIA

I have a wisteria that was planted in 1968. It never bloomed. I kept hearing stories about wisteria needing 15 years—I waited and developed a great love for its open filtering leaves that are trained over a pergola. In moments of impatience, I've tried root pruning (I'd heard that if you scare it into believing you're killing it, it will bloom) and chopping back to the ground. Nothing worked. Then I tried cutting it back to two laterals in early summer, and the following year I got one bloom. I'll keep on whacking away at it.
* Cut it back to six or seven buds after blooming (if you have blooms) and before new wood starts growing. Prune again in summer.

* To restrict the huge spread of wisteria, anywhere from 26 to 60 ft/8 to 18 m a year, in late winter prune back to just above a healthy bud; then whack it back again in late summer.

* Train as a standard—a very handsome way to use a vine. Stake the central stalk, remove all the side growth, and allow only the top to flourish. Keep it clipped so that it doesn't get out of hand. You will get repeat blooming.

Wood Ash

Wood ash provides valuable minerals for the garden, but make sure that you are using ash from real wood. Don't use ash from chemically treated fireplace logs. All you will have is chemical residue.

* Sprinkle wood ash around the base of cauliflower and onion plants to control maggots. Use them to

prevent clubroot, red spider, bean beetles and scab on beets and turnips.

* At the end of the season when nights are getting cold, sprinkle a bit of wood ash onto the soil of your plants to help them resist cold.

* Paint trees with a gravy of wood ash and water to control tree borers.

WORMS

Earthworms are essential to the health of any garden. They aerate the soil, pull leaves down from the surface, digest and then excrete manure—20 oz/580 g of castings a year—to enrich the soil. They are sensitive creatures; most chemicals kill earthworms, and without the production of worm manure for essential minerals you will have to rely on expensive, ultimately dangerous, fertilizers. They can burrow at least 6 ft/2 m into the ground and sometimes up to 15 ft/4.5 m. Worm castings produce the best of all organic fertilizers—they are far, far richer in nitrogen, phosphates and potash (NKP) than anything in the upper level of the soil. They keep the soil balanced between acid and alkaline, which is where most plants are happiest.

* If you've ever wondered why stones appear to surface as if by magic, it's the activity of earthworms. They can bury them as well. They improve soil drainage as they work their way along; worm castings hold moisture in sandy soils; worms prevent erosion and break up clumps of earth.

* Night crawlers: Most worms live below the surface, but there are some species that come out during the rainy weather; these are the ones that come to the surface at night and crawl about. They draw leaves deep into their burrows; they need lots of space and soil.

* Your compost will attract earthworms to work. When it is heating up, the red wrigglers or redworms will be doing most of the work. They do their mating at different levels in the pile rather than at the surface and at just about any time of the year. They can cope with the higher temperatures of a hot pile.

WORMWOOD. See *Artemisia absinthium*

XERISCAPING

The root definition of the word xeriscaping means no water landscaping. In practice it means designing a landscape for the minimum use of water. This should in no way inhibit your garden planning. But it does mean that you think of water, watering and all that that entails before you choose plants. To have a properly xeriscaped garden, divide it into zones and understand the culture of each area: how much sun falls on it, the grade, and the soil type. Then you will know which areas are water-retentive, and which drain quickly. Choose the plants most appropriate for the specific situation.

* Now this sounds like sane gardening, but most people start with the effect they want, a design or a color palette, before these other factors are taken into consideration.

* Once the zones have been delineated, *then* start working on the design. For example, designate plants as follows: most highly drought-tolerant plants farthest away from the source of water; those with higher water needs, closer to the water source. The resulting garden is as close to self-reliant as possible—dependent mainly on the available rainfall for water.

* In the xeriscape garden use butts to catch rain and hand water. See Rain Butts; Watering; Whisky Barrels.

* Select plants for the type of soil in the garden—acid, alkaline or neutral—rather than changing the soil to suit the plants.

* Either get rid of lawns that are great gobblers of water or change your attitude to just how perfect, how green and how often you'll feed it. If you can tolerate grass that turns brown in drought, you'll be fine.

* Choose perennials, shrubs, trees and vines adapted to your area and the microclimate your garden provides. Once established, they probably won't need to be watered again.

* Group plants with similar cultural needs—light, water and nutrients—as the foundation of your design. How you water the garden is paramount. Sprinkler systems lose 80 percent of their moisture to evaporation, which is a dreadful waste. I installed an underground watering system that never loses anything to evaporation and is used only when absolutely necessary. Of course, nothing is perfect. I'm constantly digging into the rubber pipes because I can't figure out where they are when I'm replanting. But they are easily fixed and the saving in time and water is worth it. More xeriscaping tips:

* The smaller the leaf, the more likely the plant will be able to stand up to sun and drought; any plant with gray, silver or downy foliage has a strategy to tolerate wind and drought; low-growing plants will keep themselves out of drying winds; most herbs are used to poor soil and low rainfall. And, of course, plants native to your region will be the toughest of all.

* Non-native plants from areas similar to the one you live in will do just as well: Mediterranean, Chinese,

Australian and New Zealand plants come from regions echoed in North America.

* The longer you hold water back from the lawn in spring, the tougher and deeper the root system will go. So don't baby your grass. Tough love works here. Make sure you choose native grasses rather than something exotic to give a so-called English garden look. Until we've got away from having to have Kentucky bluegrass, which needs about 18 to 20 in/45 to 50 cm of rain a year, we won't have grasped xeriscape principles. Go native and you won't go wrong. And keep your lawnmower at a high level; shearing the grass just makes a wimp out of it.

Yarrow *Achillea*

Great plant with lots of varieties. It improves its neighbors by helping their resistance to disease and bugs. Excellent with medicinal herbs.

* It makes a wonderful addition to dried flower arrangements. Cut just before the blossoms open completely, strip the lower part of the branches, then hang them upside down.

Yew *Taxus baccata*

This evergreen grows reasonably well in the shade.

Don't plant near rhododendrons, however, or the yews might succumb to root rot fungus because of the acid soil.

* Yew, with its glossy dark green needles, makes a wonderful dense hedge. It tolerates shearing well.

Zinnias

These brilliant flowers are one of the delights of summer. The scent is strange and reminds me of my childhood. They originate in Mexico and, used in moderation, will give an exotic look to a special border. Children love the intense colors, and it is easy to grow from seed. Pinch back to produce a bushy plant.

Zones

Every garden is in a specific climate zone based on altitude, mean high and low temperatures and number of frost free days. On the local level, there are microclimates in each garden, which depend on surrounding trees, how much shade is cast by buildings, and how protected parts of the garden might be. See Microclimates.

BIBLIOGRAPHY

Baker, Jerry Fast. *Easy Vegetable Garden.* New York: New American Library, 1985.

Bakuk, Paula Dreifus, ed. *Rodale's Book of Practical Forumulas.* Emmaus, PA: Rodale Press, 1991.

Ball, Jeff. *Rodale's Garden Problem Solver.* Emmaus, PA: Rodale Press, 1988.

Ball, Jeff. *The 60-Minute Flower Garden.* Emmaus, PA: Rodale Press, 1991.

Binetti, Marianne. *Tips for Carefree Landscapes.* Pownal, VT: Storey Communications, 1990.

Ellise, Barbara W., ed. *Rodale's Illustrated Encyclopedia of Garden and Landscaping Techniques.* Emmaus, PA: Rodale Press, 1990.

Goldbloom, Shelley. *Garden Smarts.* Chester, CT: Globe Pequot, 1991.

Hupping, Carol, C. Winters Tetreau, R. B. Yepsen, Jr., eds. *Rodale's Book of Hints, Tips and Everyday Wisdom.* Emmaus, PA: Rodale Press, 1985.

Lacey, Roy. *The Green Gardener.* Newton Abbott: David & Charles, 1990.

Mulligan, Bill. *The Vegetable Gardener's Answer Book.* New York: Mason, 1977.

Perlmutter, Mary. *How Does Your Garden Grow . . . Organically?* Oakville, ON: Salvation Army, 1990.

Riotte, Louise. *Carrots Love Tomatoes.* Pownal, VT: Storey Communications, 1975, 1990.

Shigo, Alex L. *A New Tree Biology.* Durham, NH: Shigo and Trees, 1991.

Simonds, Calvin. *The Weather Wise Gardener.* Emmaus, PA: Rodale Press, 1983.

MAGAZINES

National Gardening Magazine
Canadian Gardening

T.L.C. for Gardening
Organic Gardening
Horticulture
Fine Gardening
Gardening Life

In Canada, for answers to ecological questions call: 1-800-268-2000, a free organic info-line at Macdonald College, Ecological Projects, St. Anne de Bellevue, Quebec.

Index